syrian dust

syrian dust

reporting from the heart of the battle for Aleppo

FRANCESCA BORRI

TRANSLATED FROM THE ITALIAN BY
ANNE MILANO APPEL

SEVEN STORIES PRESS
New York • Oakland

Seven Stories Press
140 Watts Street
New York, NY 10013
www.sevenstories.com

Library of Congress Cataloging-in-Publication Data

Borri, Francesca, author.
  Syrian dust : reporting from the heart of the battle for Aleppo / Francesca Borri ; translated by Anne Milano Appel.
    pages cm
    ISBN 978-1-60980-661-3 (paperback)
  1. Borri, Francesca. 2. Syria--History--Civil War, 2011---Personal narratives, Italian. 3. Women war correspondents--Italy--Biography. 4. Women war correspondents--Syria--Biography. I. Appel, Anne Milano, translator. II. Title.
    DS98.72.B67A3 2016
    956.9104'2--dc23

                    2015025053

College professors and high school and middle school teachers may
order free examination copies of Seven Stories Press titles. To order, visit
www.sevenstories.com/textbook, or fax on school letterhead to (212) 226-1411.

Book design by Jon Gilbert

Printed in the U.S A

9 8 7 6 5 4 3 2 1

To Stanley Greene

"Shut your eyes and see."
—JAMES JOYCE

The most dangerous place here is the hospital. You arrive, and it's the first thing they tell you: if you want to feel safe, stay at the front.

Abandon all rules, ye who enter here. All logic. Aleppo is nothing but explosions these days. Exploding. Everything explodes and topples. And when you venture out in search of water, when you're hungry, thirsty, there's nothing but snipers everywhere. Assad's planes are suddenly strafe bombing, rushing at you in maelstroms of wind—wind, and dust and flesh. But they are so imprecise that they never bomb the front lines: they'd risk hitting the loyalists instead of the rebels.

The unit of the Free Syrian Army in which we're embedded consists of thirteen men, two in flip-flops, while the others don't always have two shoes that match. There were seventeen of them, three died trying to recover the body of a fourth man that is still out there, at the end of the street. Their base is a school, and each of them has a Kalashnikov and a knife. In the principal's office, a child polishes the family silver: two rocket launchers and a rifle. Except for the captain, an officer who left Assad's troops six months ago, they're just young kids of seventeen, eighteen. Alaa is studying philosophy, and between shifts he reads Habermas. Deserters are easily recognizable: they stole their camouflage shirts from the barracks. The others wear T-shirts sporting Messi or Che Guevara.

The Syrian Spring has turned into the Syrian War. And the evolution can immediately be perceived in the difference between the Lebanese border and that of Turkey. Beirut is a refuge for the most notorious activists: the ones who started it all in March 2011, demonstration after demonstration, protest after protest. The ones from whom the Free Army, in a sense, seized the revolution. They not only helped us journalists cross the border illegally, but, more importantly, they enabled us to understand their motives and demands. Now the border with Lebanon is inaccessible, however, guarded mile after mile by Hezbollah's men. Allies of the regime. On the other hand, the border with Turkey has been opened: the rebels control the passport office, a doormat at its entrance portraying Assad. But this new Syria of which they are the self-appointed spokesmen is honestly an unknown. Difficult to discuss politics here. Useless to inquire about UN negotiations, about Islam. About Sunnis and Shiites. For the rebels, the main thing is to have us fork over $300 apiece: the fee they charge for a tour of Aleppo under attack. Journalists are the big business of the day.

Because, in theory, there are four fronts. But the truth is that there is only one front here: it's the sky. And those who have nothing but bullets to use against the fighter jets haven't got a chance. Without intervention from the West, as in Libya, the Free Army can't win. And so, for now, it's trying not to lose. They're defending positions in Aleppo, nothing more. They're not advancing.

On average today, at al-Shifa hospital, there's been one death every three minutes and thirty-seven seconds. To reassure the population, the rebels drive around in jeeps rigged out with Dushkas, old Soviet machine guns, but a machine gun placebo against a fighter plane has about as much effect as a peashooter. Most importantly, to reassure the world—to convince it that they are deserving of weapons and support—the rebels drag the rest of us to the front, exposing us to invisible loyalist snipers. Two, three of them crouch at the first intersection, a hundred yards away. Then they dash across, upright, blindly spraying rounds with the Kalashnikovs. Up and down. As cameras flash. When they cross back, when they return to our side, they don't ask if they've hit the enemy. They ask: "How did the photo come out?"

Every so often, doubling as stunt men for themselves, they forget to release the safety catch.

Meanwhile everything around is exploding: exploding and collapsing. As soldiers play, children die. There should be civilians and combatants in Aleppo, there should be a front—a here and a there. Instead there are no rules. There's no asylum. Ambulances are loaded with ammunition, mosques converted into military posts. Refugees in the barracks, explosives in the fire extinguishers, undergraduates at the front working on their dissertations, students at the university bombed while in class. Mines in the parks, corpses among the swings. Rebels wearing loyalist uniforms. Loyalists without uniforms. And this base we're settled in looks more like an occupied high school than an army unit. It's one continuous fight. Whose turn to cook, how to capture the next block. What tactic to use. You stole my boots, no, you're the one who stole my blankets. And it's only a microcosm of what happens among the various armed groups, and more generally speaking, among the various opposition groups. Because the Free Army should eventually hand over its power to the National Council, that government-in-exile of sorts based in Istanbul, but there is no sole leadership and no sole strategy. Neither among civilians nor the military. And this, more than any arsenal, is Assad's real strength.

In and out of the classrooms, amid the Kalashnikovs and grenades, there are children running around. Ahmed is six years old. "Today I'll teach you to be a true Syrian," the commander tells him. "A free Syrian." He hands him his Beretta and makes him fire a shot in the air, in these narrow streets flanked with eight-story buildings, their windows already smashed in. Another one shatters. A woman, her hair in a braid, skirt down to her ankles, runs out frightened. The bullet got wedged in her kitchen. She grabs my pen and notebook. "What kind of Syria will ever emerge," she writes, "from men like these?" And she goes back to her cubbyhole under the stairs.

A HAND PULLS me to the ground, and the bullet, a few feet overhead, rips into the wall.

I'd wondered where the inhabitants of Aleppo had gone. There are over two million of them, according to the latest census, 2,132,100 they say, and two-thirds seem to be still here, in these rubble-strewn streets besieged by snipers. But the houses, blasted by artillery fire, are empty: a lamp, a curtain, fossils of normal lives dangle in the wind from structures left gaping, torn open by the bombs. Even a cat here, curled up in a chair, appears to be sleeping, but it's dead.

I'm in a dark hole when I get up, a steep flight of steps in front of me. And there they are, finally, Aleppo's inhabitants. Dozens of shadowy wraiths shuffle around me, curious; I'm the first soul they've run into in two months. A cigarette lighter casts a glow. Nineteen children, clinging tightly to one another, stare at me in silence, lined up against a wall. Frozen. They look at me terrified, then I see why: it's the helmet. They think I'm one of Assad's soldiers. They're lined up against the wall like prisoners awaiting execution.

The house of Umm Bashar was hit right away, at the beginning of August. She should really be called Umm Mahmoud, the mother of Mahmoud, since Bashar, twenty-eight, the firstborn, ended up under a hunk of concrete, his sweatshirt sleeve sticking out, scarlet, in the dust. They had to run away because the bombings, in general, occur in twos—the second is meant for the rescuers. There are thirty-seven people in here. Five men and thirteen women, plus the children ranging in age from one to nine. All they have with them are the clothes they were wearing when they fled. They can't afford to rent a house, nor do they have fifty dollars for a car to the Turkish border. So they get by down here, a camp stove in the corner and no water, gas, or electricity. Every now and then Omar, twenty-nine, a taxi driver, ventures out in search of food. Across the street there's a sniper waiting for him. Omar's brother Shadi, twenty-seven, a mechanic, was killed that way. "I'll never forget the day I found myself sifting through the vegetables. The sugar, the rice, whatever he had bought. Washing the blood off the potatoes, and cooking them anyway."

At this point, inside or outside really makes no difference in Aleppo. The entire city is pounded by aircraft, helicopters, and tanks, hammered inch by inch: bombs and blasts, an explosion every few seconds. Thousands have sought refuge underground. "They hand out bread at the cemetery. Only among the dead can you be certain of not being a target," Omar says. But the truth is that there is no safe haven: since Assad unleashed the use of airpower, survival is a matter of luck. "On the outskirts high-rises protect you from mortar strikes. You go to the first or second floor: maybe only the upper floors will collapse. If a plane hits the building though, you're left under tons of rubble. In a one-story house, on the other hand"—he means the kind typical of Aleppo, graceful homes with a central courtyard, lemon trees, jasmine vines—"in a one-story house, unless the plane strikes right on top of you, there's less rubble. Maybe they'll dig you out. Though there's still the danger of mortars."

The truth is that the only safe thing to do in Aleppo is leave.

Except it's our turn again now. An anti-aircraft machine gun abruptly spits out three shells. And it's an instant, that's all. Just time to look at one another and that's it. An Assad fighter jet starts roaring in our heads, its black shape, through a vent grille, appears, disappears, reappears, levels out, climbs again, nineteen children screaming frantically. These are the cruelest moments, because the mind is still lucid. And as the pilot chooses his target, while maybe it will be you, all you can do is huddle there, your back against a damp wall, and stare at the floor along with everything you've left undone in your life, everything you put off, as you look around, now that maybe your number's up, and even if you had something to say, here among these strangers, anything you could utter, any name, any wish, any regret, whom could you say it to? now? no matter who you miss, no matter who you once loved, surrounded by these dark eyes, the hunger, the mud, this feverish skin, these haggard faces, surrounded by these lives that are not mine, this plane coming back, and they ask you: Are you all right? But the truth is that they don't even know your name—and all around you, meanwhile, there's bombing.

Aisha, nine years old, hands me a business card. An address: it's the shop above. The one the stairs lead up to. "Tariq al-Bab," she says, "we are in Tariq al-Bab. Write that they should come and get us. Don't write useless things." Then she notices my phone, and asks: "Do you have the number for the UN?"

Yet, as battered as the city is by Assad, Aleppo's underground is wary of the Free Army. "They started a war that they were not prepared to fight," Afraa, sixteen years old, tells me, that one sentence marked by four explosions. "There they are with flip-flops and ten bullets apiece," she says, "we will be crushed. They gave Assad exactly what he was looking for: an excuse for violence." When you ask about the rebels, opinion is almost unanimous in Aleppo: no one knows what their strategy is, or who they really are. And worst of all, what kind of Syria they want. Afraa has taken part in dozens of demonstrations. "But that's all over now. Now it's time for arms. We have no place anymore, no voice." Seventeen words, five explosions. "They take our houses, shoot from our windows. And they don't care if we have no other place to go. If we are trapped. In two months, we haven't seen anyone here." Not an NGO, not the Red Cross. Not a Doctor Without Borders: no one. Another mortar rains down. The crash of shattered glass. Screams. "Besides, they are all so religious, all so conservative. And all Sunnis," Maryam says. She is Afraa's best friend, and she too is all in black. But she's Christian. She points to her veil, and tells me: "It's my helmet."

I keep looking at my watch. Waiting for dawn. But I'm the only one; it's a habit from the old life. Because the only difference between night and day here is that without light the Kalashnikovs are useless. At night, all that remains is the metronome of explosions. The rebels can't respond to that. At night in Aleppo the war becomes slaughter. You don't fight, you die and that's it. Randomly.

They bomb here, they bomb and bomb. That's all.

FORTUNATELY, Abdel Qader al-Saleh is a very busy man and only has ten minutes for the journalists. Because he's the commander of the rebels in the Aleppo zone, and to show that he is not afraid of Assad or anything else, he arranges for his interviews to take place on the front line, wearing a short-sleeved shirt and holding a glass of tea. "I would say that the situation is positive," he begins. An explosive burst nearby. "Another two months," he assures us, "and Aleppo will be liberated." Another explosion. A building at the end of the street, already buckling, gives way completely. "Maybe three." The dust covers us. "Another biscuit?" and he pours you more tea.

Actually it's been twenty days now since his men launched the conclusive offensive for the conquest of Aleppo, after the conclusive offensive in August, and the only difference is that the front lines are now the front zones: there's fighting everywhere. The city, or more precisely its ruins, is a maze of snipers, hammered by artillery. Until the night before, the rebels claimed they had no more ammunition. So it seems they decided to go for broke, a moment before surrendering, and attack. It's rumored that they were counting on mass desertion among the regime's ranks, arranged through some of Assad's officers—that is, bought from some of Assad's officers—for thousands of dollars. But after twenty days, no one has advanced here. It's just a new balance point on a higher level of violence. "But don't write that no one is advancing," a doctor at al-Shifa counsels me, holding what look like bloody plaster flakes in his hands. "The numbers of dead are advancing." I rashly offer to throw the flakes away for him. They turn out to be skull fragments.

The narrow section of the front where we are embedded is an intersection in the old city populated by three interpreters, seven photographers, two journalists, a cat, and four insurgents. Around the corner, a loyalist sniper. The four rebels sit in what must once have been a small shop, engaged for the past hour in a lively discussion of strategy for the capture of Damascus. An elderly woman, meanwhile, with a basket of vegetables, emerges cautiously; she lives across the way. But no one pays any attention. And after a while, resigned, she crosses by herself, mumbling verses from the Koran as prayer. Even Wikipedia recommends what's called "covering fire." That's two dollars a bullet, Fahdi chews me out, "are you crazy?" And he goes back to planning the capture of Damascus. In the afternoon, reinforcements jump down from a jeep in the person of Ayman Haj Jaeed, eighteen years old. Today is his second day at the front. Write this, he tells me: "Assad is at the end of his rope." He crosses the street at a run waving his Kalashnikov, shooting as fast as he can. "Write, write!" he yells at me from across the street: "Two more months, and Aleppo will be free." Only he fired to the left. And the sniper was on his right.

The rebels all have similar stories. They're laborers, engineers, truck drivers. Students. Shopkeepers. They've seen
Tunisia on television, they've seen Egypt, and they too have
begun to protest. Demonstration after demonstration. All
peaceful. But meanwhile the police went from handcuffs to
bullets, and from bullets to tanks. Because the rebels all have
similar stories. They all started out that way, peaceful, until a
father, a brother, was killed, and they joined the Free Army.
"Don't call it a civil war," they keep telling you. "We are not
Syrians against Syrians, but Syrians against Assad." And then
they ask you: "Why doesn't the world get involved?" Dollars
arrive from other countries, mainly from Qatar and Saudi
Arabia, but not weapons. The United States vetoes it: they
don't have confidence in these rebels who lack organization
and direction, both military and political. Who lack everything. Their press spokesman here, Mohammed Noor, can't
even tell me approximately how many insurgents there are.
And besides that, General Riad al-Assad, the commander in
chief of the Free Army, isn't even in Syria: he's in Turkey. He
communicates with the commanding officer via Skype.

But above all, the Free Army has a hard time winning
international support because it is estimated that between
eight hundred and two thousand men, 5 percent of the total
number according to various research institutions, may be
traced back to Islamic fundamentalism. And in fact the battle
here began with twin car bombs claimed by an Al Qaeda
group. It was February 10, 2012. And one of Aleppo's most
active brigades today, the Ahrar al-Sham, the Free Men of
the Levant, is aimed explicitly at forming an Islamic state. It
is also one of the most recognizable brigades, whose fighters
wear a black band on their foreheads reading: "There is no

other God but Allah and Muhammad is his prophet." In
the streets under the rebels' control, it is not uncommon to
come across loyalists being dragged by the hair, drenched in
blood, bearing the unmistakable signs of beatings and torture.
"But Syria will be a democracy," the rebels assure you. Until
a mortar suddenly rains down. "We will respect everyone," a
second mortar, then a third. I dive into the first doorway I
can find. Except those inside are all men and I'm not wearing
a veil under my helmet. It will be a free and equitable Syria,
they keep saying, but for now they leave me outside.

They are Libyans, Iraqis, Chechens, Afghanis. Yet they are
not the only foreigners in the Free Army. Because in reality
that's what Aleppo's inhabitants consider the rebels: foreigners.
Aleppo is the economic capital, the Milan of Syria. A wealthy
city, with a mixed middle class, Christian and Muslim, Sunni
and Shiite, not many differences—a city of industrialists and
entrepreneurs, all focused on business. Its contribution has
been marginal in the demonstrations of recent months; the
war came from outside, when Turkey opened the border and
Aleppo, for the rebels, was the first stop on the road. The Free
Army here is not like it is farther south, not like in Homs, in
Hama, where a young man, a father, defends his own neighborhood, the block his house is on. The rebels here are Syrians from
the countryside, poor Syrians, who accuse the people of Aleppo
of indifference, cynicism, opportunism. While the latter accuse
them of destroying the city without having the slightest thought
about the future—except for a future of sharia, moral law, in a
country where Sunni Arabs, however, make up only 63 percent
of the population. A week ago, three of the rebels ended up at
al-Shifa hospital, not wounded by bullets, but by glass bottles.
Not hit by snipers, but by irate citizens.

The rebels have no anti-aircraft and the bombing is non-stop. But over Al Jazeera, Riad al-Assad urges them not to worry: the forecasts predict fog and rain for the next few days.

ASIDE FROM A Widows Brigade whose members are not further identified, apparently operating near Idlib, the only female rebel we have any definite information about is Thwaiba Kanafani. A forty-one-year-old architect with two children, she moved to Aleppo from Toronto, Canada, arriving in flawless makeup and high heels, ready to enlist in the Free Army. "No one suspects a woman," she explained in dozens of interviews, "so I engage in spying—I'm here undercover," she posted on Twitter. Complete with photographs.

The delegates of the new National Council, elected this week, to whom the rebels are supposed to someday hand over power stripped from Assad, are all men. "But it's not true that women do not have a role," those at the Free Army's press office inform me. "They too have responsibilities and duties," Mohammed Noor tells me. "Her, for example"—and he points to a middle-aged woman holding a bucket and rag: "She's head of the janitorial unit."

Mona and Ghofran are sisters, twenty-three and nineteen years old. We're at the front, machine guns hammering a sniper's nest across the street, sandbags, blood-soaked mud, a house in flames—a mortar has just exploded—and two black *niqabs* emerge through the dust like a hallucination. "You see?" Wahed, the interpreter, says to me, satisfied: "It's not true that women are kept shut up in the house." Actually, it's the first time that Mona and Ghofran have ventured out in two months: they've run out of money, and they have a sick father. In the meantime, three chairs and three glasses of tea appear—in the middle of the street, amid the bullets. "And then you write that we don't respect women," Wahed says. And he hands me a biscuit. Mona and Ghofran have no idea what's happening in Aleppo, they don't have electricity. They have no television and no telephone. They want to get across the city and reach an uncle to ask him for a loan. "We have nothing, I'm sorry, not even a lira," Wahed apologizes. Meanwhile he has my $300 daily fee in his pocket. Plus Giulio's $300, and Javier's $300, Zac's $300. "You don't need to interview me to understand," Mona says. "Assad is a criminal, no one doubts that. Look around you." All around, in fact, there is nothing but rubble. Remains of houses, remnants of walls. Among the tangled sheets of metal, a dog: in his teeth, a tibia bone. "We've taken part in dozens and dozens of demonstrations. But now, with the war, women are excluded from the revolution. Sure we have a role: being among the dead."

Osman al-Haj Osman, a surgeon at al-Shifa, the only hospital that's still active, is frustrated. "The female doctors and nurses have all gone. They're afraid. And we are forced to do triple shifts." Because, it's true, there are five doctors here, all men. But of the nineteen nurses, nine are women. "When the revolution began, I had just graduated," says Zahra, twenty-four years old. "This is my internship." Amid the thousands of mortars that have struck al-Shifa, she's been wounded three times. "I keep telling myself that I'm here for the freedom of my people. But I know full well that even if Assad were to fall, for me freedom would still have to be won. I prevented an amputation for my father, who didn't want me to go to university. I rolled up my sleeves so I wouldn't infect his arm, and I sewed him back up, with everything vibrating from the explosions, all around, with a corpse beside us, and with my father protesting: 'Cover yourself!'"

Because the air in Aleppo is dense with gunpowder and testosterone. "The men claim we don't have courage, that we are too emotional," adds Bahia, she too twenty-four years old, she too wounded three times. She too still here. "But I'm not so sure that lack of feeling, in some cases, is a sign of rationality. Passing your time at the front in flip-flops and repeating that you're protected by God: it doesn't seem so normal to me. The only way not to be afraid is not to think. Which is, however, also the best way to ensure that this war will never end. And so true courage, in Aleppo, is not to get used to it. To be afraid: to think." In Raqqa, a city to the east, toward Iraq, it was the women who offered themselves as human shields. Against the rebels, though: they asked them to spare the city. But general Riad al-Assad was adamant: "It is necessary that we liberate you," he said.

Meanwhile, at the entrance to the hospital, a car dumps a body. That's how bystanders mowed down by snipers arrive. Picked up in the street and unloaded here in front by a car that races off, since al-Shifa is under constant artillery fire. At times, the body is hit by mortars even before it's dragged inside. "And it disintegrates, literally," Bahia says. "Dust. Dust amid dust. All of Aleppo, by now, is a monument to unknown citizens."

After twenty months, 35,000 victims, and 450,000 refugees, the map of Syria is appalling. The Free Army controls the area of Idlib, to the north, and little else. Some pockets in Aleppo, pockets along the road to Damascus. Pockets infested with snipers, however, and flattened by Assad's bombings, hour after hour. "And on Syria's ruins, they will plant the flag

of fundamentalism," Bahia accuses. She is a believer and prac-
titioner who wears the veil. "But my Islam is not their Islam,"
she explains. "Fundamentalism? What fundamentalism!"
Osman interrupts her. "We are all doctors here, all equal:
men and women alike." His father was a leader of the Muslim
Brotherhood. The whole family was forced into exile. Osman
grew up in Saudi Arabia, and came to Syria for the first time
three months ago. Every night he goes back to sleep in Azaz,
on the border with Turkey. The first city to come under the
authority of the rebels, and more specifically of its imam, as its
self-proclaimed spiritual and political guide. "It's up to you to
participate, it's up to you to earn a place," Osman says. "You
are free to do anything. Even to perform surgery."

"Even to govern?" Bahia snaps back.

"Even to govern."

"Even to fight?"

"Even to fight, of course." And everyone around laughs.

The screech of brakes. A car spits out a black bag on the
asphalt, and takes off again, tires squealing. Two eyes stand
out, white, against a *niqab*, pupils upturned. It's Mona's body.

IN ANY CASE, people must have heard that there's a war
around here, they must have gotten one of those text messages from Save the Children, "A Euro for Syria," because
we're back in Turkey, and in Kilis, on the border, everything is
booked. Hotels, restaurants: all famous journalists.

I got Jason Alison, from New Zealand television. This is
how it works: they appear at breakfast one morning, and in
addition to the assorted drivers and interpreters and hair-
dressers, they hire one of us freelancers as a guide. They pay

your $300 and all expenses, and besides that you learn a little about the craft. Because Jason is New Zealand's leading war correspondent. He has thirty years of experience, and for me, thirty years old, period, he's a gold mine. Except that he's an expert on Africa, especially Rwanda, he's an expert on Rwanda and the Balkans, and he's only been to the Middle East once, on vacation. And he bought a carpet, a carpet and a teapot, and so the first question he asked me was whether I could summarize who is opposed to whom and for what reasons. And I must have involuntarily given him a somewhat puzzled look, or astonished, or appalled, because he hastened to tell me that of course he knew where we were, we were in the midst of a civil war, Syrians against Syrians. Then he said: "Sunnis against Shiites," and added: "The Shiites are the ones who follow Ali, right? That has to be explained, that they are the followers of Ali, otherwise my viewers will be confused." And he made a note in his notebook: Check on Ali.

His cameraman, a certain Mark, is also here to learn the craft. He's twenty-seven years old, and this is his first trip outside of New Zealand. He even bought a *Lonely Planet* guidebook. He showed up in a bulletproof vest and Bermuda shorts. That's how he arrived in Aleppo: in shorts.

But they're a gold mine, those veterans, so I keep quiet and listen, and try to learn. Because it may not seem so, but here everything is questionable. For example: the flak jacket. The word *Press*. Because journalists, it's true, shouldn't be a target. On the contrary. But since they killed the Japanese reporter Mika Yamamoto in August, aiming specifically at her, not a stray bullet, well—maybe it's better to take off your press tag. Only many of us are in favor of it because of the insurance: if you don't have the tag—if you look like a civilian and they shoot you—the insurance has a clause by which they won't pay you. I think it's Paragraph 22. And so we talked for two hours and sixteen minutes today, and after retracing all the conflicts of the last twenty years, in particular the theory and practice of the Hutus and Tutsis, we finally decided to consult one of the combatants at random about the tag. Who emphatically advised us: "Definitely. Use it. Always." Then he asked: "What does *press* mean?"

The second thing I learned is that I should not say "regime" when I'm talking about the Assad regime, because if I do I'm not being neutral and not respecting everyone's views. I should say "the Damascus government"—even though, truthfully, it's the government of Damascus that's pounding us, and it's not that I don't want to respect the opinions of others, but I would also like to respect international law sometimes. And as far as international law goes, I'm afraid the government of Damascus is a regime. In any case, the third thing I learned is that you have to go searching among the dead to find interesting stories. The dead and the wounded, and possibly women and children, because otherwise the viewers won't identify and they'll change the channel. And it's honestly not clear to me why a New Zealander should iden-tify with a Syrian woman with seven children, only one arm, and a husband in Al Qaeda, but anyway: Jason has thirty years of experience. And so we roam around all day looking for the dead and wounded, and my role, specifically, is to ask Khaled, who is the interpreter, and for whom I translate from English to English, that is, from Jason's native speaker's English to an English that is understandable, things like: I need a mutilated orphan. Or: I'm missing a child hit by a sniper in school. And of course: a boy soldier, possibly drunk—"There were some in Sierra Leone, there were some in Chad," Jason protested yesterday, threatening to fire Khaled, "You can't tell me there aren't any here."

And so, in search of what we call "real life," and what the editorial and cutting room staff call "a little color," we spend hours and hours at al-Shifa, because the regime, that is, the government of Damascus, is always there, doggedly trying to demolish it. Grenades, bombs, mortars. Whatever. Casualties arrive every minute at al-Shifa. All torn up, all dust and blood, tatters of flesh, relatives around them screaming desperately, fainting, beating their heads against the walls, bodies on the ground, among them one or two still breathing, amputated hands, limbs that someone carried here so that they might be reattached, only now no one remembers who they belong to. And in the middle of it all, as always, these young kids in white coats: because everyone has to help as best he can in Aleppo, even children. Mohamed Asaf is twelve years old, Yussef Mohammed is eleven. They are on duty from 8 a.m. to 8 p.m. They disinfect, bandage, suture. They console. They extract shards, inject morphine. Sometimes you go in at five in the morning and they're still there, among the decapitated bodies, a leg on a stretcher, some fingers on a chair. But they're still there, mopping the floor in the light of dawn, when even the last of the dying dies, like when you walk through a deserted city, and people are washing the sidewalk in front of shops that are still closed, early in the morning, and the pavement, outside, is all water and soapsuds. Mohamed and Yussef mop the floor like that, in that same silence of a spent day that is already beginning again, the pavement all water and blood.

And I honestly wonder: What's the point? At night, when I'm there watching the New Zealand news broadcast, and all

I see are dead bodies, bodies and grief, despairing mothers, and maybe it's Syria, maybe Iraq, maybe it's another war, I couldn't say: all I see are dead bodies. And I wonder. I think of Cassese—since our feature today was called "The Failure of Aleppo." Cassese was my professor of international law. He was also president of the Hague Tribunal, the tribunal for former Yugoslavia, and he always talked about the BBC, about the time the Serbs seized six UN trucks and the BBC explained that the distribution of humanitarian aid in Bosnia was blocked by the collapse of law and order. And Cassese would say: "Have you ever seen a truck blocked by a failure?" "Verbs," he said, "have a subject. Actions have responsibilities."

Actually another story aired tonight, because the production editors noticed a couple of bullets whizzing by: a sniper. And so the news tonight was us—the attack on a New Zealand television crew—even though we hadn't even heard the bullets. And even though the death count here today was 137. There was bombing at some point, we ran into a basement, there wasn't one free inch of space. A man saw the TV camera and said to me, "Your life is more important than mine," and he gave me his spot. He went outside. Amid the mortars, gunfire, choppers, and all the rest, he gave me his place, explaining: "So the world will know."

TO HIS COMPANIONS he is simply Qannaas, the Sniper. A sharpshooter who, in February, decided to desert and joined the Free Army. No one knows his real name. He comes from a military family, from a town near Damascus, and his uncle is still a general in the service of Assad. His brothers, cousins: they're all high-ranking officers. And all of them, except his parents, think he is dead. Qannaas prefers it that way—partly because he really is a little dead.

He has short black hair, a beard, and he's twenty-one years old; he's a skinny guy, with a stare that's both intense and inexpressive as he waits in steely silence, motionless, for hours, finger on the trigger, eyes on the gun-sight. He calmly picks off anyone who steps in front of him. A clean hit, short and sweet, not so much as a twitch afterward. Only a cough. Eyes again on the viewfinder. He only gets irritable when he talks about the war. Because the war, he says, is changing. "Many aren't here to overthrow Assad, but to acquire fame, notoriety. A reputation. To have power when the war is over." And he's not the only one in Aleppo who thinks that. Many tell you that the war will continue once Assad falls. They say that if Assad falls, fighting will begin between secularists and Islamists, or between Sunnis and Shiites. Muslims and Christians. Or, more simply, between the various armed groups: purely over control of territory. Purely for power. "But Syria will not become like Somalia," Qannaas says. "Worse, we will have a Somalia in every province." The war is now unrecognizable, he says. Then he takes a breath. A deep one. "By now, we are unrecognizable."

It all started with peaceful demonstrations. In March 2011, when dozens, hundreds, then thousands of Syrians took to the streets demanding political and economic reforms. Liberty and dignity. They didn't even want to overthrow Assad at the beginning. They just wanted reforms. But Assad responded with violence. Immediately. He said it was an American conspiracy. That the demonstrations weren't genuine. He claimed that they were filmed in a studio. That it was a set of Al Jazeera in Qatar. And he reacted with growing violence. And in July 2011, in the wake of Libya, the Free Army appeared, proposing to serve as a frame of reference for a transition to democracy, and hoping to convince the West to intervene. Only something went wrong—basically because Gaddafi had no one anymore. He had no more allies, only business associates for his oil, only buyers, while Assad had Iran and Russia. And most importantly, of course, Assad didn't have oil. But all in all, things did not go as the rebels expected, no one intervened, and now here they are making catapults from street signs and explosives out of ammonium nitrate from plant fertilizer and tinfoil, like pages out of the Junior Woodchucks manual. Increasingly forgotten with each passing day, increasingly on their own, they scavenge for resources as best they can, and in particular wherever they can, namely outside of Syria, from nations or private citizens. They do it, naturally, by promising loyalty to their patrons in tomorrow's Syria. "But all they buy is our temporary gratitude," Qannaas points out. And ultimately Syria becomes more entangled with each passing day here, because not only do the weapons increase, but also the objectives for which they are used.

In part because the rebel advance has meanwhile ceased, and by now can no longer be measured by cities, or even neighborhoods, but by blocks, as the war hibernates in a war of position: a war fought by men like Qannaas, guys fifty yards away, facing each other, trading insults all the time, sometimes shooting, sometimes chatting, when they discover that they know each other. In the end that's how it is in the Middle East, they're all relatives and cousins, and you're there for your piece on the Sunnis and Shiites while they're fighting over Real Madrid and Barcelona.

Qannaas studies the walls, considers the best spot in which

to station himself, and between one place and another pours some food for a fish that is still swimming in its glass bowl. Today he's on duty in the old city. Where the rebels are fighting from these elegant houses, lined with books, the curtains embroidered. Chandeliers, velvet sofas, and them. Coming from the countryside, they always feel somewhat in awe amid all that inlaid furniture, the hand-painted tiles. They're afraid of breaking something, they move around timidly, uncertainly, here where everything, all around, is exploding—exploding and collapsing. The owners of this apartment must have fled in a hurry. They left everything. The fish, toothpaste on the brush. Half their dinner still on their plates. In the other room there's some artillery and a corpse, purplish; two other snipers carefully pack up all the ceramics, the silverware, a painting, while a third sniper, on guard duty, stands barefoot at the door so he won't ruin the carpet.

Of the thirty-four he's killed so far, Qannaas simply says: "They were *shabia.*" In Arabic that means "ghosts," slang for Assad's plainclothes militia. They have plagued the Syrians for years, and today *shabia* is the most frequently heard word in Aleppo. You get the impression that even your wife's lover has become a *shabia*, or the boss who hassled you, the customer who has never paid his debt. Or those you've killed though you're not sure why. Like Mohammed, Qannaas's closest friend.

"We went to school together. We grew up together. His mother is like a mother to me." And together they enlisted in the call-up. Mohammed was the only one who knew that Qannaas wasn't really dead. "I told him to desert, and he replied: 'Not yet, it's too soon.' I told him that I would help him. That I would hide him. But he kept saying: 'No, not yet.'

He was afraid that what happened to my family might happen to his." That is, interrogations. Threats. Ostracism, neighbors not talking to you anymore. "My family was spared the worst," says Qannaas, "only because they are all officers of Assad— and because everyone thinks I am dead: really dead."

Mohammed was stationed at the Shatt checkpoint, and Qannaas had warned him: that checkpoint was their next target. "But he didn't listen to me. There were three of us. We killed a colonel, a soldier, and Mohammed. I don't know which of the three I killed," he says. "All I know is that we had enemies in front of us. And they ordered me to shoot."

He takes a deep breath. Being a sniper in Syria is the job that's most in demand. And the highest-paid. "We'll be able to buy ourselves a house when it's over," he says. "If there are any houses still standing." It's the highest-paid job because it's the most difficult job. No, not because you have to be precise, he says. "Because you see your victim."

THE FIRST STRIKE exploded unnoticed, as did the second, covered up by the screams of a young boy, his leg torn off, as a doctor closed it up just like that, without anesthesia, using a kitchen knife for a scalpel. But the third hurtled down on the other side of the sidewalk, crashing into three bodies waiting to be identified. The fourth demolished a wing of the building across from us, the fifth a wing of the building beside us, as we realized that al-Shifa was again under attack.

Blasts of plaster flakes, shrapnel, and glass, the dust rising like a tide, dense, filling the air, and this rumbling, louder and louder, closer and closer—like a vise, the artillery gradually closing in around you. The mortar is a rudimentary weapon that doesn't allow you to calculate distance. You can only choose the direction. Then someone, close to the target, says by radio: farther east, farther west. Someone who is close, at this moment, and who is watching you. But in Aleppo an artillery attack is also a hail of bullets. Fired into the air, fired at the ground. Fired everywhere and anywhere. And completely pointless: the mortar launcher is miles away. But the purpose is to convince us that we are protected by the Free Army. And so, in addition to dodging mortar shells, you also have to dodge the rebels, who have been taught how to shoot, though no one explained when.

Alaaeddin, the driver, yanks me away, shoves me into the car on top of three other journalists and takes off, breaks squealing. In a panic, because it makes more sense to take refuge in a basement, behind a wall, to flatten yourself on the ground, anything, at this moment, except to be out here on the street as the road suddenly disappears behind a curtain of dust. And in the midst of it this car, blind, zigzagging drunkenly. An explosion to the right, an explosion to the left, while we, inside, retreat under our helmets and watch our death play out on the windshield, like at the movies, as everything around us topples, collapses, and burns. Only the snipers are left. A car in front of us swerves. Then another, a man rolls out and is struck in the head. Once, twice, there on the asphalt, the bullets drilling into him; with each bullet the body jerks, twitches, shudders, and Alaaeddin drives faster and faster, more and more disoriented, until a helicopter appears and he turns left, then right, down narrower passageways, the chopper descends, closer and closer, choosing its target as Alaaeddin slams a parked car, goes right again, then straight, bangs into another car, makes a left, another left, a right, a left,

and screeches to a halt: we're back at al-Shifa again. "Shit,"
he says. And squeals off. We reach the Turkish border, thirty-seven miles, without a word. Blood from al-Shifa on our
boots.

Alaaeddin stops just before the passport control. He says:
"I'll buy some water." We get out too, amid swarms of children hoping for a coin, a biscuit. A shot, in the distance. We
unfasten our helmets. Another shot. The border is a camp
by now. A third shot, a fourth. There are already 140,000
refugees in Turkey; the border is closed. Another shot, then
another, a burst of Kalashnikov fire—and we realize we are
under attack. Alaaeddin yanks me away again, hurls me into
the car, and we turn back. We head toward Azaz, which is
the first city the rebels captured: it's under their complete
control. We're safe there. Amid the remains of a mosque, the
charred husks of the regime's tanks, pictures of the battle in
the park at town hall. The war in Azaz is already a museum
piece. Meanwhile, we have no news of Aleppo. Nor of Narciso, who is still at al-Shifa. The only news we get is from
the wounded on their way to Turkey. The old city, they say,
is in flames. Giulio stayed back there. So did Javier. You can
hear the echo of explosions. Aleppo is on the horizon, to our
right, the deep orange of sunset scored with black and red—
it looks like lava. Another conclusive offensive must have
begun. Alaaeddin stops near the pharmacy. He says again:
"I'll buy some water."

We get out too. Helmets on the hood.

A man gives us bread.

For a week we had only tea, in Aleppo. He gives us bread
and oranges.

We gaze at the sunset, to our right.

Alessio is also over there.

When a plane, suddenly, rips the air.

And as always, there's no place to take shelter, no basement, no wall, nothing. Nothing. Nothing. The bomb hits a house three hundred yards away. "It's over, if only for today," Wahed says. And he runs off to help the wounded. Another explosion: another bomb.

On the same house.

What can I write? Plato has already written it all. Only the dead have seen the end of war.

THEY RAISED FUNDS for stray dogs. To build a kindergarten in the Congo, a well in Ethiopia, to rebuild a church in Haiti. To save the wolf and the bear from extinction, and the blue-fin tuna as well, to finance cancer research, stem cell research, for a hundred polio vaccines for a hundred children in Afghanistan. To plant a tree in Nigeria. They told me: Berlin has heart. It's receptive and liberal. I left some small change for the dog people. The woman asked me: "Where are you from?" I said: "From Syria." "Oh," she said. "Syria." She said: "Syria must be lovely. But it's a little difficult now, isn't it?" she asked. Indeed—you could say that, ma'am. Sixty thousand deaths, four hundred thousand refugees, oh yes: Syria is a bit difficult at the moment. A missile can come along and incinerate you. Blood in the streets, bits of brain and guts, yes ma'am. A sniper might pick you off. "Oh," she said. "I never imagined." Then she said: "Just think how many stray dogs there must be."

And then she said to the guy next to her, the plant-a-tree guy: "Do you know she's come from Syria?" "Oh," the tree guy said. "I adore couscous. Have you ever tried it made with fish?" Then he questioned: "But you're not Syrian?" "No," I said. "I'm a journalist." "And you're in Syria?" "In Aleppo." "Oh," he said. "Aleppo." He said: "Awesome." That's just what he said: "Awesome." I told him: "Every now and then someone dies." He said: "Better one day as a lion than a hundred days as a sheep."

A week ago, while I was waiting for the commander at the school that serves as the rebels' base, as I was putting my notes in order, there were two children chasing each other around from one classroom to another. At a certain point I turned and one of them, who must have been around six years old, was standing in front of me with a .22 caliber pointed at me. The safety off. He was playing. My one hundred days as a sheep.

I am in Berlin for a prize. The UNICEF Photo of the Year Award. Which for 2012 obviously goes to a photograph of Syria, because what could be more dramatic than Syria this year? Even though, truthfully, neither UNICEF nor the UN have ever been seen in Aleppo, and the only thing they organized for this war was Kofi Annan's special mission: an attempt at negotiations, which began in February and was shelved in July. If you look for news of it on the Internet, the only remaining trace is how much it cost: $7,923,200. $3,022,300 went to salaries.

The UN also sponsored this award and the prize went to Alessio. Alessio Romenzi. Someone who, typical of our generation, repaired broken-down refrigerators in a provincial life as sung by the 883; then he left Italy, and in two years found himself on the cover of *Time*. Alessio is blond, fair-skinned, frugal, shy, and introverted, a man of few words. A person who, if he has something to say, will send you a photo from his iPhone. "But then at night," says Andrea Bernardi, a cameraman who has been in Syria for months, also at the front, "you hear him talking in his sleep about bloodshed and battles." And Andrea is another one like that: he talks about everything, but never about the war. "Because they tell me I'm nuts, that it makes no sense," he says. "That if I need the adrenaline rush, I can parachute instead. And it's no use explaining that not only does someone have to be a witness to all this, but that I'm not a thrill-seeker. I don't defy death: in Syria, in Iraq, in Libya, when everything might be over in a second, nothing is more powerful than life."

Well anyway, I'm here partly because I got an infection in Aleppo, and I've had a fever for a month now. And partly because these photos were the images that made the world aware of Syria: and me too. It was February 2012, and Alessio had covertly crept into Homs through the water pipes, while the city was under siege. And he took these photographs that, when you look at them all together, one after the other, make you see clearly what Syria is today. And not only Syria; you realize what freedom is, and dignity, and courage. Yet that's not the reason why I was so moved, the reason I bought a ticket for Beirut and decided to write about Syria. The real reason, actually, is that Alessio is someone who had worked all his life, whereas I'd spent years studying for one degree, then a Master's, then another degree, and yet I'd never understood Syria. I'd never understood a thing until I saw those photos in front of me. On the contrary. Everything I'd studied proved to be completely unfounded. Completely useless. Beginning with Kosovo, where I started out, which was supposed to be a humanitarian war, right? A just war. A war of the left. It began as a war to defend the Albanians from the Serbs, but when I got there, the problem was to defend the Serbs from the Albanians—somewhat like the peacekeeping mission in Lebanon, which had been presented to me in thirty different courses as a peacekeeping mission par excellence. The perfect operation, just the kind you should carry out, should you become secretary of the United Nations someday. You should do the very same thing, they told you: it's so perfect, in fact, that it's been thirty years and it's still in place. And Lebanon too: still on the brink of collapse.

And basically I would like to be able to write like that, and above all to live like that: like Alessio's photos. With that immediacy, that naturalness—that depth. And I came to Berlin. Philip Roth was once asked to name the most important book he'd ever read. And he replied *If This Is a Man* by Primo Levi. Because after reading it, he said, no one can ever say he hadn't been to Auschwitz. Not that he hadn't known about Auschwitz. No, that he hadn't been there. The power of that book—it's the power that certain photos have. They grab you and take you there.

Only I'm at this strange ceremony now. In the midst of this reception with wines that cost as much as it does to feed twenty families, or to pay for twenty cars to the Turkish border, and to tell the truth, it makes an impression. Because there's this photo at the entrance, the photo that won the award, and there it is, life-size, and it's the picture of a little child. A little girl dressed so that she looks like a doll, one of those porcelain dolls: all embroidery, a pleated skirt, a flower in her hair. And I was there when it was taken, because it was taken at al-Shifa. Her father is beside her and the little girl is holding her father's hand. And she has this look of fear, but more than fear, bewilderment, this questioning look, and it's directed at all of us, all of us here in front of her, this look as if to say: I don't understand why this is happening. And plainly the picture is beautiful. And yet—it has a strange effect. And not just because of what was around her, outside the picture, forgotten now, because children aren't frightened in Aleppo, they're torn apart. The real photos never end up in the newspapers, so as not to be insensitive, so as not to offend people's sensibilities, and you don't even submit them, you keep them for yourself, the real photos, along with your ghosts, along with the words you say only at night; but no, it's not just because of that. It has a strange effect because after this it's time to take pictures—photos for the press releases, time to take photos with the photo—and there they all are with those stemmed wineglasses, those patent leather shoes, those ties, all so elegant, those smiles, and they have this photograph in front of them, life-size, this little girl, yet nobody tells them: She's dead, see? Because, meanwhile, on November 22 al-Shifa was blown away, and everyone was killed. The doctors, the nurses. All of them. The patients, Osman, Zahra Bahia, everyone, and the little girl, the little girl too, there's been no further word. She was the doctor's daughter, that little girl with the flower in her hair, and they are all dead, blown to bits, strewn everywhere, and they are all covered with maggots now, putrefied, rotted, food for the rats, all still under there, the little girl too, where did she end up? And that's what Aleppo is like, outside the picture, that's how it is, where nobody cares about these little dolls in the rubble, these rag doll bodies amid the worms, the rats.

A dog occasionally unearths a bone.

An American approached me. An official of something or

other. "It's a tragedy," he said. "A real tragedy." And he stared at the photo. He said: "It's a real tragedy. A tragedy that's difficult to deal with, so many aspects, that ancestral hatred, and Islam, a tragedy. Problematic." I said: "Yes." He said: "Difficult. Unfortunately, it's a time of crisis. How can we intervene effectively? We don't have the resources," he said. He said: "The wars multiply, resources shrink. In some offices we no longer even have paper for the printers."

Then he said: "It's just a tragedy."

And he poured me some wine. He studied the glass against the light. A Cabernet. He said: "It's a red that's unmistakable." "Yes," I said. "Unmistakable."

Like the snow on the ground in front of al-Shifa.

Every morning, a family loads everything into a van and returns home. The one in front of me, nine children, three women, two men (two brothers who took part in a demonstration against Assad in October were killed, only a scarf of theirs remains amid the rubble), is going back to Al-Bab, near Aleppo. They will be bombed in six hours.

But anything is better than the refugee camp at Atmeh. Even war.

A few feet away from Turkey, with laundry hung out to dry on the barbed wire marking the border, more than thirteen thousand displaced individuals, haggard and emaciated, wander among tents that often aren't even tents, but simply sheets of plastic, sheet metal, old flour sacks cobbled together, a tattered shirt to plug up a hole, fetid carpets on the ground, soaked by now as rain pounds on the walls and drips on them. No electricity, no gas, no water, only a fierce wind-driven snow. And for latrines, a dozen holes in the ground hidden from view by piles of bricks. The shower is a mother, a sister, who hands you a pitcher amid ankle-deep sludge. All they have is what they were wearing when they fled under mortar fire. Children drag through the mud in adults' shoes, a sweat-shirt and little else, their eyes sunken. They have no firewood either—the olive trees in the fields around here are guarded by the owners—so they burn branches, leaves, empty bottles of the mineral water a truck unloads, at dawn, along with stale bread. Sometimes a little rice. A few potatoes. There's nothing else.

Now that Aleppo is bogged down in a battle in which no one advances, journalists move on quickly from Atmeh. The rest of the country is inaccessible, studded with the regime's checkpoints, and for many reporters the refugees' plight is the final story before catching a plane to Mali. A few distracted lines, a few lines because you have to—because of the children. Yet Atmeh speaks of much more than its hardships. More than the cold and hunger. Because in Atmeh, unlike the city's basements, there are only rural makeshift trenches, there are only refugees now, or corpses, the only Syrians you meet in Syria.

You enter Atmeh from Turkey, from the Turkish border city of Reyhanli. Where every day a new agency sets up its headquarters. In Syria it's a heyday for the NGOs, since the UN, through the UNHCR (the Office of the UN High Commissioner for Refugees), deals with refugees who cross the border: almost 650,000 in Turkey, Lebanon, and Jordan. And 100,000 more in just the last month. As for those displaced within Syria, no one has any idea how many there are or where they are. The regime does not issue visas to foreign NGOs, so the entire territory is open to Syrians themselves, everything subject to improvisation. Many of them, out of the country for years, have flocked here to set up their associations. That is, to print a business card and rake in donations.

"The problem," explains Adi Atassi, "is that there are no defined roles." In Cyprus he's a street artist, and here he is in charge of refugee emergency services for the National Syrian Coalition—an alliance, based in Istanbul, for the coordination of opposition groups against Assad. "If you need anything, you don't know who to turn to. But the disorganization is intentional. Because Atmeh is a historical junction point for smugglers: this way, in exchange for kickbacks for aid, they can continue to have control over the territory for other types of trafficking. Everybody has an interest in Atmeh being a no-man's-land. Everybody, unfortunately, but the refugees."

The National Coalition was established two months ago, in November 2012, replacing the National Council. The latter had been formed to act as a beachhead for Western intervention, as in Libya, to have an alternative government ready for when Assad might fall. But first it became divided on the timeliness of a Western intervention. And then on whether to overthrow Assad with armed force. And later on whether to overthrow Assad at all, or maybe to seek a compromise. And then on a thousand other things. And ultimately the international community, not being able to change the opposition, thought to change its name. Every so often a delegate pops in among the tents, and in preparation for an election distributes a few biscuits to the refugees, like a tourist feeding the pigeons in Piazza San Marco.

The one who dropped by this morning came from Paris and is very concerned about the winter. About the snow. He's wearing Clarks. Pointing to the suede, he says, "The stain won't ever come out."

In Istanbul they're already planning for the post-Assad period. But first you have to live long enough to get to that time,

and in Atmeh you can end up burned to a crisp by an unat-
tended candle. Nine victims. Because the cold here tightens its
grip on you day by day. And you have to have seen the beauty
of Damascus, of Aleppo, at least once, the elegance of a Syrian
home, the carpets, the rose-filled courtyards and pastel painted
tiles, the wrought iron lamps—you have to have seen all that,
of which nothing remains but photographs on cell phones—to
understand Atmeh now, to understand the despair, the reversal,
the hopelessness of this regression to the Stone Age, warming
yourself around the fire, depleted, wrapped up like beggars in
whatever you've been able to scavenge, your child shivering,
filthy, his hair like stubble, a garbage bag for a diaper, that dull,
ashen expression, exhausted, burned-out eyes, the hunger, and
not even a toilet, the humiliation of crouching in a field like
cattle. They talk to you in trailing phrases, head bowed, like
Karim who cuts himself while trying to fashion a can of paint
into a stove with his bare hands, a trickle of blood barely oozing
through his muddy fingers. All he says is: "I am ashamed."

At sunset we simply retreat to our tents. Stomachs empty,
in the dark, without a word, an average of 10.8 people to a
tent, though in this one there are twenty-three of us, lined
up like bodies in a morgue, sleeping fully clothed, huddled up
in old tattered blankets. With old fears, new hallucinations: a
car tears by, racing, and suddenly it's the shriek of a fighter jet.
And it's an instant, that's all—just time to look at one another:
that's it. Time that hangs suspended inside you again, waiting
for the explosion, again: it's death at your door.

In six months, we haven't seen anyone here. Not the UN,
not an NGO. Not the Red Cross: no one. Only the Saudis.
Who are the main financial backers of the rebels, but who also
assist civilians. They come and fund a family. For $300 they

buy a bride. "It's not speculation, it's generosity," claims Ismail, forty-one, who has just chosen Layla. In fact, it all takes place in the light of day—or rather, in the shadow of tradition. Layla is fifteen years old. Her father died of leukemia, and she's here with her mother, eight brothers and sisters, her mother's parents, aunts and uncles, and assorted cousins. Deciding for her is her mother's father. And he decides unilaterally. "Layla knows that I know what is best for her," he says brusquely. Layla's consent is not necessary. Nor her opinion. She looks at me, while her sisters, around her, shorten her dress, try on makeup. She looks at me and doesn't say anything. "I would have liked her to study," her mother whispers. "But with this $300 her brothers and sisters will survive."

Then she says: "It's true that it's a tradition. I was thirteen, my husband thirty-one."

Then she looks at the ground, and murmurs: "But it's a male tradition. Write that down."

Mahmoud Najjar is twenty-four years old, with a degree in English Language and Literature; the stamp of his old life can be seen on his jacket, tailor-made shirt, and Diesel jeans. "The majority of Syrians were opposed to reacting to Assad's violence with violence. It was inevitable: it would only destroy the country and any international solidarity. The Free Army has dragged us into a war that it is incapable of fighting. It has reduced us to beggars," he says. "And that's not the end of it." Because in reality the Free Army, with its twenty-year-olds and their Kalashnikovs and flip-flops, their tinfoil and fertilizer grenades, is now the rear guard compared to those who have stepped up as the special forces of the revolution: the Islamists of Jabhat al-Nusra. The Support Front. Branded as terrorists by the United States, they are mainly foreigners, like the Iraqi who commands the unit guarding the refugees in Atmeh. And who will not speak with a female journalist, only men, and possibly only non-Western men. "In the liberated areas, the transitional government consists of Islamic courts in which someone pulls out the Koran and calls his own will justice," Mahmoud says.

The jihadists are the ones who enter through Atmeh. That's why international NGOs are not allowed to operate here. They don't want anyone inconveniently looking around.

And that's why the Syrians are increasingly fed up, tired of both Assad and the rebels.

The National Coalition, in all this, comes to blows over the formation of a government in exile. Its sixty-three members are all long-time dissidents of the regime, who have been living abroad for a lifetime. To be interviewed, they don't even leave a Turkish phone number, but one that's French, American, British. They're nothing more than foreigners by now. Them too. Like those who are fighting this war and those who have come back to make a profit. "They're interested in Syria," Mahmoud says, "not in the Syrians."

The only one who doggedly persists in dealing with the Syrians is Bashar al-Assad. He even bombed Atmeh. And thirteen thousand people made a dash for the border, screaming, terrified. Pressed against the barbed wire. One on top of another, cornered with no way out, hunted down to the last, even as they were: barefoot, starving, ankle-deep in mud. Hunted down just like that, even four-year-old children.

IT SOUNDS LIKE a plane approaching, and—it's just an instant—they all look at each other, words stuck in their throats. But it's only a gate sliding closed. An ax splitting wood is a Kalashnikov's burst, the clack of a woman's high heels on cement the abrupt shot of a sniper. We may seem normal in Aleppo, but fear is a disease that is eating us up inside.

Seven months since the start of the battle, only one thing hasn't changed here: Assad's fighter jets are so imprecise that they still never bomb the front lines. Earlier their favorite target was al-Shifa hospital. Now that all that's left of its walls is dust, all that remains of its doctors is a framed photo and flowers, the most dangerous places are the bread lines. There are only women and children this morning. About two hundred of them milling in front of a mosque vie for a handful of cartons with a little oil, rice, chickpeas. Some sugar. They're missing fingers, ears; those beaten eyes on you, haggard and emaciated, a tattered sweater and little else against the sting of winter's biting wind, skin parched, worn, on the bones, on the jutting shoulder blades and cheek-bones, taut like wax. The mothers see you, a foreigner, and try to leave their child in your arms. "Take him with you," they tell you, "save him."

And there are many children at the demonstration in Bustan al-Qasr as well. The river that bisects the neighbor-hood and marks the border between rebel-held Aleppo and the regime's Aleppo spewed out dozens of corpses a few days ago, each with a bullet hole in the neck, wrists bound, mouths taped shut. All civilians, all returning from this side. The youngest was fourteen years old. The Aleppo across the river, the regime's Aleppo, is also the well-off Aleppo of the bour-geoisie. Where you can still buy things. And so, from here, people cross over by the hundreds every day. Over there they sell TV sets, clothes. Whatever you want. And when they have nothing left, they sell fish, at a price that's sky-high, given that the riverbanks are rife with snipers.

If they find you in Assad's Aleppo—if you are a male old enough to fight and they find you—you disappear.

The Free Army expects half the city to march today. Instead there are only about a hundred kids. Popular resistance no longer exists. No more activists. The city is worn out. They don't even have gas. The van with the megaphone is pushed by hand.

The woman in front of me has sallow skin, and a name that she repeats three times but that I don't understand, because she has no teeth. She's a widow, and has two daughters in their twenties. And I can't figure out what she has on her feet either, something strange. Like pieces of cloth, only it's not cloth, it's fur. She sees me looking at her and says to me: "Cat fur." It's from the strays they dine on. Because they've fled to the industrial area of Sheik Najjar, to a house that's under construction, four pillars and a cement roof with walls of jute fiber, and the only one working is one of the daughters. In a still functioning factory, near here, that produces snack foods. But with her salary they can only buy a package of bread each per week. Little more than a slice a day. The rest is rainwater. And cat meat. "But one night we heard three men arguing heatedly. Then a shot." The corpse is still there, three hundred yards away. A stain in the grass. "And now the cats are eating its body."

She looks at us. She asks: "But eating rats is dangerous, don't you think?"

Not even the guy from the Free Army who is with me has ever come across such a thing. He takes off his scarf, his jacket, his cap, he rummages through his pockets looking for coins, he's even about to take off his shoes. But the woman says harshly: "I don't want anything from you. It's your fault."

The Free Army entered Aleppo in August 2012, counting on a general uprising. "But not only were they under the illusion that they could win a war with a handful of bullets. They think they own the city. Houses, shops: whatever they want, they go in and take," Marwan, an attorney, tells me. "They're no better than Assad's soldiers." He has a cut on his eyebrow, a black eye. Yesterday, at a checkpoint, he tried to protect his wallet and phone. "And worst of all, if they hadn't used schools and hospitals as their bases," says his brother Radwan, an engineer who now teaches mathematics, "Assad would not have had an excuse to bomb everything." Along with some friends, Radwan has set up a school in an apartment. We are in Mashad, three hundred yards from the front. The only light in the classroom is an LED tube, the kind you use to decorate the balcony at Christmas time. Hearing the rumble of mortars, the children don't even turn around. Only when there's a hail of bullets do they start dickering: "It's a Dushka," says Ahmed, six years old. "No it's a short-barreled Kalashnikov," says Omar, six years old as well. "Hear it? It's lighter than a Dragunov."

Some have turned to teaching math, others have become doctors. Many of the wounded are treated in private apartments, without electricity, by the light of cell phones or cigarette lighters, a carpet for an operating table, a cutter for a scalpel.

Because in seven months, still no one has been seen here.

Not the United Nations, not an NGO. Not the Red Cross: no one.

After a night of below-zero temperatures, the windows

without glass so that they won't shatter in case of an explosion, being in Aleppo means washing yourself with melted snow at dawn, sharing two apples among nine people, and feeling fortunate that you're still alive. The only activity is trying to warm up. It's freezing: bitter cold. So cold that you're purplish, your skin rubbed raw by frost. The Syrians have cut down every tree, every shrub; we scour the ground searching for anything that can burn and give us a blaze, one second of warmth, old tires, old slippers. Although, truthfully, nothing here is more frightening than the sun: bad weather is the only anti-aircraft protection.

Everyone is always looking up at the sky in Aleppo. As the mind quickly considers the options. Wherever you need to go, whatever you have to do, whatever the place, you try to assess the probability that it may be bombed. You try to reason it out. You think maybe a neighborhood that has never been bombed is better. Because you think that maybe it isn't a target, that maybe the regime doesn't care about it. Then you think, maybe not. Maybe, on the other hand, it's more likely to be bombed now, since it has never been bombed before, right? And so you choose a neighborhood that's already been bombed. But then you recall those that have been bombed two, three, five times, and you find yourself making these calculations, these assumptions, that throw you into a spin. Maybe one that's been bombed twice is better than one that's been bombed six times, or maybe the one bombed six times is better, because how many more missiles can hit it? What's the probability? And no matter what you think, the truth is that it's best not to think. Because you think that maybe a market is safe, because a slaughter at a market would remind the world of Sarajevo; it would be going too far, even for Assad.

But maybe it's the opposite. Maybe attacking a market would suit Assad, just because it's going too far: because it would convince Aleppo to surrender. Like with the gas: because in August Obama said the use of gas was the red line. He said that if Assad used gas he would intervene, and now you never know if you're safe or maybe not, if someone from the rebel forces will use gas to force Obama to step in and . . . you realize that everything is unpredictable, that you can't even be prudent, you can't even minimize the danger, because a bread line is as dangerous as the front; you realize that one option is as good as another, because everything is a target; you realize that nothing makes any sense, that maybe one minute you're alive, then maybe not, incinerated by a missile that you won't hear coming, and you're completely alone, completely vulnerable, in this city, this life your reasoning doesn't have the slightest influence over, the slightest grasp, completely adrift, hostage to things you don't understand, and maybe in a minute it will all be over, just like that, by a fluke, after centuries of science and the Enlightenment, strategies, logic, books, studies, Bacon and Galileo; and where do you go now? after man went to the moon, after physics, chemistry, which path do you take? which is safer? after they told you that everything had an explanation, a formula, a cause and effect, after we can manipulate nature, after DNA, after Kant, and now it all ends like this, by a fluke, and there's no logic, there's nothing to hold onto, and as I write, maybe I'll die, maybe not.

Incinerated by a missile that I won't hear coming.

Anyway, Aleppo, in theory, has a government now.

The mayor's name is Jalal al-Khanji, age sixty-seven; he's an engineer, and he presides over the new Revolutionary Council, elected by the city's notables. His office is in a bank on the outskirts, and he has one priority: bread. A package, eight slices, used to cost fifteen lire; today it costs two hundred. Almost three dollars. To provide essential services, namely waste management, electricity, water, and, in particular, bread, Aleppo requires about $10 million per month. In all, they've received $1.3 million, essentially private donations, with just pennies from the National Coalition, to which Kuwait, the United Arab Emirates, and Saudi Arabia just added a check for $900 million.

"The majority of the funding goes to finance the political activities of the opposition. But food and medicine are not just humanitarian aids in Aleppo: they're political. More important than a thousand meetings in Istanbul, a thousand conferences," the mayor says. "Because otherwise families here would have no other choice but to turn to the Islamic brigades. From them, bread is never lacking."

Jalal al-Khanji's office is completely empty.

Not a pen, not a sheet of paper. Not a stamp. Not one clerk.

Were it not for Jabhat al-Nusra, in fact, it would already be over here. And it's not just a matter of bread. Al Qaeda's men are a minority, about 5 percent of the combatants, according to estimates, but they are the best trained, the best equipped. They are the ones who decide. In a short time, they've captured almost all the military bases in the surrounding area, almost all the artillery batteries. The regime attacks with planes and missiles, while the Free Army's General Headquarters in Aleppo is now the General Headquarters of Jabhat al-Nusra.

Not much is known about them, however. They don't talk to us journalists. Though, by contrast, we talk about nothing but them. With their black balaclavas, Jabhat al-Nusra is the most picturesque subject we could hope for. Some even have a saber, and naturally those are our favorites.

But the truth is that Aleppo keeps its distance from them, focused only on surviving. Rumor has it that Jabhat al-Nusra promised the Free Army that they will leave once Assad falls, once law has been established. That this is the agreement. "What they mean by law, however, isn't clear," Salem tells me, puzzled, having just reopened his fruit and vegetable kiosk. "They deserve respect: without them we would all be dead. But Syria is and must remain a plural, secular country." Salem has a piece of shrapnel in his arm. A grenade's handiwork. "They'd stopped me because I had a bottle of liquor. The grenade exploded while they were warning me about how dangerous alcohol is."

Down below, beneath the General Headquarters, they have set up a prison.

But nobody knows anything about the detainees. Who they are, and how many. And why they're there.

On what charges they were arrested. If they will stand trial. If they will be executed.

You ask. All they tell you is: "They are *shabia*." Ghosts.

SHE ARRIVES AT work in the morning, veil and a trace of mascara, and parks in front of the door as if she were going to the office. But it's the only thing left to her, from her old life, because that's not the entrance to the high school where she teaches English, but the door to her sniper's post.

She's thirty-six years old, and has had a new name for the last six months: Guevara. Her two children, Wael and Mira, died in an air raid. They were ten and seven. And she enlisted in the Free Army. "They were so terrified by the war. The bloodshed, the explosions. And I tried to reassure them, I kept telling them, I kept saying: I'll protect you." She looks at me. "I'm here to avenge them."

The unit she fights with, about thirty men, is called Wa'id. The Promise.

Two years, sixty-five thousand victims, seven hundred thousand refugees. But Guevara receives us warmly. "Welcome!" She slips the pistol into her handbag and offers us coffee on an old couch, as composed as if we were in the kitchen of her home. But we are right on the front line, behind a pile of bricks and sandbags. Two hundred yards farther on, a cordon of white buildings: that's where Assad's Aleppo begins. That's where his snipers start. Where bullets rain down.

Guevara's post is across the street. On the third floor. But it's not as close as it seems: to dodge enemy fire, she leads us through basements, from building to building, between breaches ripped open in the foundations. Then she simply enters, sits down at the window in a living room, the dinnerware still intact behind her and two plants, now withered. She waits for someone to stumble into her crosshairs. She doesn't show the least bit of emotion. Only when she spots a Snow White blanket from the hallway, in what must have been the children's room, does she hesitate for a second. "I know what you want to ask me. Whether I ever think about it, about my former life. But for two years you've been watching Assad's carnage, indifferent to it. The real question is this: You who judge me, what alternative have you left me?

"It's not as if you find yourself at the front all of a sudden. I've always been an activist. But at some point you realize that demonstrations are useless: it's your megaphone against their tanks. And if we don't want to be killed, everyone here must help as best he can. Being a sniper, if you ask me, is the best role for a woman, because it's a matter of concentration and precision, not strength. I know I'm an exception. My girlfriends, at most, volunteer as nurses. But caring for our wounds is not enough. We must stop Assad from wounding us."

She's not surprised, really, that women in Aleppo are not at the front line. It's not just the traditions of Syrian society. Guevara admits: "They all know and respect me here, but I know what they're saying, that my husband should be the one to defend me." That's not the point: the point is the Islamists. More and more of them. And more and more radical. Truthfully, they don't seem to consider women particularly useful. "But that's the very reason why it's important to be here. Fighting. To be able to matter more in tomorrow's Syria," Guevara argues. "At first, my comrades were wary. I gained their trust in the field," she says. "Bullet by bullet.

"All those who are an example began by being an exception."

As she sees it, any Syrian who hasn't joined the Free Army is a traitor. That includes the rest of her family, who live three hundred yards away: beyond that row of white buildings. Father, mother, and nine brothers and sisters. "Aren't you ever afraid you'll hit them?" I ask. Partly because the criteria for distinguishing civilians from enemies don't seem very exacting. "I shoot those in uniform," Guevara explains, "and those who seem suspicious to me." Those who come by at night, for instance, or who pass by several times. "It's not that I'm certain. But if you choose to remain on the other side, to stay there and watch, you are basically supporting Assad. Silence here doesn't make you a spectator: it makes you an accomplice. It's not that I'm unafraid. But when I wake up with a start at night, and I wonder how we ever ended up this way, I just whisper to myself: Mira! Wael! Because in spite of everything, I will remember these days as the best days of my life: as the days I won freedom."

She has hit what she calls "the target" twenty-five times. Five died.

"And when I hit them, I wait. Because after a while, someone comes to recover the body. And I shoot again, without thinking about it. Because my only thought is that promises must be kept."

EVA, MEANWHILE, has arrived in Turkey, in Antakya, our base city, less than twenty miles from the border. A slight, gentle lady from Genoa, extremely thin, with long, straight pale hair. Big, frightened eyes. She smokes one cigarette after another, trembling all over. She's shaking so much that you have to fill her teacup half-full, otherwise it spills on the floor, on her notes, on her datebook, which looks like a seismograph. Because her son said he was coming here on vacation, at Christmas, and instead he went to Syria to fight with Al Qaeda.

He's twenty-three years old, his name is Ibrahim. That is, I don't know his real name: Eva doesn't speak with journalists. "I don't want to end up on the front page. Or to have my son discussed on talk shows, by people who are football experts one day, cooking experts the next day, then experts on Syria. An opinion poll to decide if he's more of a terrorist or more of an idiot. And a showgirl telling me where I've failed as a mother.

"For you, he's just another young man," she says, "For you, my son is an exclusive worth thousands of euros."

And I don't know what to say to her.

Because I'd like to say that it's not true, and yet it is true. Of course it's true. Because it would end up on the front page tomorrow: an Italian boy, fully Italian, meaning not second generation, not the son of immigrants, a young Italian, in Syria. At the front. And not someone from a rural village, but someone from Genoa, with a mother like Eva, just like your own mother, someone just like your son, holed up in his room on Facebook, and who knows who in the world he's in contact with, what he's thinking, what he's harboring inside. I'd like to tell her it's not true, but the truth is that these types of things are just what the newspapers are looking for. A European jihadist, a sniper in spike heels. Simplifications, caricatures. Black and white, this is wrong and that's right, these are rational, those are deranged. All the rest, the context, doesn't matter to them. Your motivations, what you are, but also how you became that way. The front, but also why you went there. The newspapers don't care about Syria, they don't even know where Syria is. The other day one of them asked me: "Will you write me a piece about the clashes amid the ruins of Petra?" and I didn't have the heart to tell him that Petra is in Jordan. They only want things like these, the child doctor. And the child soldier, possibly drunk.

And so I don't know what to say to her.

Eva may spend half an hour with you, then she'll meet you ten minutes after you've said goodbye and won't remember who you are. She doesn't remember anything. She's distraught. So they all avoid her. They think she's crazy. "I don't want to get involved," Lorenzo says. "Let her call the Farnesina,* the Red Cross. 118. I don't care," he says. Lorenzo is the veteran, the one who's been here the longest. The one who knows the rebels best of all, from one brigade to another: who does what, who's stationed where. Who's who. But when he runs into Eva, he crosses the street. But I'm from the South of Italy, and those words, in the South, have a disturbing sound. Those words are not my words. And then I simply think—my father. I think my father would be here just like Eva is, exactly like Eva, with that cup filled halfway and those notes that look like a seismograph. Because he's the type who waits downstairs until you turn the lights on in the house, in case the elevator should get stuck with you in it, and your cell phone might not work because of a sudden electrical storm. Assuming that you haven't plunged down the shaft meanwhile, that the doors haven't opened without the elevator being there: a hypothesis my father never discounts.

Well, anyway—I think about my father.

I think: she's not crazy, she's normal.

That maybe she's the only normal one here.

And yet I don't know what to say to her.

"He was studying at the university, then he dropped out. He was looking for work but couldn't find a job." Eva doesn't tell me anything else, she doesn't trust me. She only shows me a picture of Ibrahim, in case I should see him in Aleppo. A tall young man, with a beard. Tunic. But honestly, they all look like that. I'd never recognize him.

And it makes me a little sad really. Because you sense that she's separated, that she and Ibrahim's father don't speak to

---

* The Italian Ministry of Foreign Affairs.

each other, not even now. At one point she discovers that his father has heard from Ibrahim via Skype, yet she only found out about it three days later. I try to tell her that her son doesn't have enough experience, that even if he was trained, he certainly wouldn't be at the front, because the Islamists take the fighting seriously, they don't lounge around the intersections of the old city in flip-flops. And so, if he's still alive, it means he's not at the front. After all, it's not as if everyone fights. I try to tell her that maybe he's in logistics. A guard at the ammunition depot. Maybe he's the one who uploads videos to YouTube. But honestly, in Atmeh, or even on the flight to Antakya, at the airport, they all look like that: tracksuit and duffle bag, but you can tell from the beard, or from a missing ear, that they're jihadists. All the young guys look alike. The ones who are looking for a job and can't find one. For months. Years. And there they are, wandering around aimlessly, with this feeling inside of being useless. And a father doesn't let the mother know he's heard from him when he disappears for three days. For three months. With this feeling inside of uselessness. If I were to see him, it's true, I'd never recognize him. He's identical to a thousand others.

CONFIRMED, in the end. After three days of yes, maybe. No. But then again.

They killed Abdallah. Ten yards from the Media Center.

He was shot from behind.

Abdallah is Abdallah Yassin. He was thirty years old, and without him, many of us would simply not have written anything here. He'd fought briefly with the rebels. But then he preferred the role of activist. There were six brothers, all of them

in the Free Army: two dead, two at the front, and two at the
Media Center. Which had been set up by Abdallah. And which
was none other than his own home at the beginning. We all
cooked in his kitchen, slept and worked on his carpets. Worked
for hours, and each time you looked up, he would refill your cup
of tea. We all raced through the potholed streets of Aleppo in
his white jeep that sported the colors of the revolution.

But Abdallah was much more than that. Because unlike the
others, he wasn't only concerned about practical things. He
could transform a washing machine into a stove. Recharge a
battery with an electrical cord and a lemon. But he had set
up the Media Center because he was convinced that international support was crucial to defeat Assad. And that to
gain international support, Syrians had not only to tell the
world about the regime's crimes, but also to explain their own
thinking. To convince the world to trust them. To intervene.
Assad's Syria but also their own Syria. "All I read about are
the dead and wounded," he would say. "The number of bombs
today, where, what kind, how many buildings collapsed, how
many tons of rubble. Sometimes," he'd say, "I read, and I think
I'm reading the stenographer's log in a police station, not a
newspaper."

Then he'd say: "My freedom depends on you."

He'd say: "Your iPad is more powerful than my Kalashnikov."

And then he'd tell you about Syria. He'd tell you about the
regime. What life was like. The persecution, the brutality. The
fear. The first demonstrations, back then, the clashes. He'd
tell you about the rebels. The strategies. The hopes. But also
the regrets, the mistakes. And he'd tell you about the Middle
East. The context.

Because Syria is complicated.

Assad's first reaction to the Arab Spring, on January 31, 2011, came in an interview with the *Wall Street Journal*. Ben Ali, in Tunisia, had already fled, and Mubarak, in Cairo, was under siege in Tahrir Square. But there was no hesitancy in his voice, no uncertainty: "Syria is different," Assad declared. "In Syria it will not happen." And in his own way, he was right.

Two years later, he is still in power. Because Syria, certainly, is similar to many of its neighboring countries—to Egypt, to Tunisia. It has 22 million inhabitants, 60 percent under twenty-five years of age, and tens of thousands of college graduates condemned to unemployment by an atrophied economy in a now saturated public sector, a legacy from alignment with the Soviet Union. While privatization in recent years enriched the Assads and their most loyal friends, state resources dried up along with oil reserves. Agriculture, once the source of 25 percent of Syria's revenue, was decimated by drought. According to estimates by the UN, 10 percent of the population was not only below the poverty line, but also below the line of survival: a dollar a day—one day being the time it took for Assad's wife, in March 2012, with the war already underway, to spend $450,000 on lamps and sofas. This is why Syria is complicated. Because it's a regime at the end of the line, like many of its neighboring regimes. Because it should already have fallen.

It's not just a matter of military superiority. Of missiles versus bullets.

The problem is that the Assads, from the time of Bashar's father, Hafez, who became president in 1970 with the last of a long series of coups, have above all been synonymous with order and stability; in exchange for freedom, of course, in exchange for one policeman for every 153 people. Whereas Lebanon, which is just a few miles from here, with its thousands of religions and its thousands of wars, has always been a warning to everyone. And one of the most ominous. The majority of Syrians, in fact, 75 percent, are Sunni Muslim, but minorities are abundant, and most of all diverse. Christians, Alawites, Kurds—with Christians alone broken down into eleven communities.

"The specter of Lebanon," Abdallah used to say: "This is Assad's real strength."

But two years and seventy thousand deaths later, Assad's strength, it's now clear, lies elsewhere: in the opposition. The Free Army doesn't have the slightest affiliation with the National Coalition. "What they think doesn't interest anyone here. And not just because they live in Paris, London, New York. But because they've always considered Bashar, who became president in 2000, a young cosmopolitan reformer, held in check by officials inherited from his father along with the country. Someone who wanted to renew Syria, but was hampered by the old guard. And therefore not an enemy, but on the contrary, an ally for a peaceful transition to democracy. They have always sought collaboration. Even now. Compromise. They've always favored stability, despite the fact that each of them has a personal history of imprisonment and persecution."

Despite the fact that the president here is the commander of the armed forces, the secretary of the Ba'ath—the one and only party—and the chief executive. He appoints the prime minister, the government, the highest-ranking civilian officials, and the highest-ranking military officers. He appoints the judges. "The only real law is the state of emergency. It allows the arrest of anyone suspected of constituting a threat to public order. The only stability in Syria is that of oppression."

Because Syria is complicated.

And now everything is even more complicated than before. All the more blurry. More muddled. A month ago they bombed the university. Which is in the regime's Aleppo. But still today the dynamics aren't clear. You can't figure out who it was. The rebels say it was one of the regime's jets, of course, while the regime says it was rebel rockets. It says they were aiming at a military academy nearby. It was a day of exams in architecture: eighty-three deaths. But in the video, you hear only two explosions. Then someone tells you it's a plane, the other says rockets. How can you not even be sure about that? A plane or rockets. A plane over your heads, did you see it or not? That's what Aleppo is like. That's what this war is like: confusion. The university is overflowing with the displaced, not just students: thirty thousand people are living there, but no one wants to admit that either. The regime wants to deny that there's a humanitarian crisis; the rebels want to deny the fact that people from districts they control are taking refuge in districts under Assad's control.

With each passing day, everything grows more complicated. More equivocal. The warring groups multiply, the National Coalition is divided—and Abdallah is killed.

The most diverse rumors are going around. Some say he was killed in a brawl. Some say he was killed for unpaid debts, or for money issues in any case.

Because journalists are beginning to be big business in Syria. And not only for the $300. The news is no longer hush-hush: Jim Foley has disappeared. After Austin Tice disappeared in August.

They've started kidnapping us. The other morning three French reporters were also seized. But they were quickly released: Abdallah had called the Free Army and provided the names of those who ordered the abduction and those who carried it out.

A few hours later he was killed.

It's pointless to ask the others. Lorenzo, as usual, cuts you off: "I don't want to get involved," he says. Because this war is changing, but we too are changing. There are fewer of us every day. The front is stalled, and by now the photos—which are what counts, because the stories, for the newspapers, amount to zero—the photos have all been seen by now, they're always the same. And the deadline for awards has passed, everything has already been submitted. For the World Press Photo, the Robert Capa Medal. And every day there are fewer of us. Every day someone tells you: "Why stay? There's nothing to write about. Go to Mali." Although it's not true that the war is languishing. The front is stagnant, but all around the front everything is changing. And the war is not the front, it's all the rest— everything behind the front that generates it. Except that it is infinitely more difficult to analyze. To interpret. It takes time. It takes study, it takes patience. It takes intelligence.

And it takes individuals like Abdallah.

None of us went to his funeral.

I left seven red roses at the spot where he was killed. The Media Center was deserted. Only his brother was there. The Canon still on the table, the sweatshirt. Cigarettes. Silence. There wasn't any electricity. Only the sound of mortars outside. Not very far away. A blast of dust and smoke from one of them, and I huddled in a corner. The same corner where I'd huddled in October, on a night when Aleppo was an explosion every few seconds, relentless, the dead and wounded everywhere that night, one of those bombings whose sole objective was to leave no one unscathed. And I was there alone. On this same carpet. Too dangerous to reach the others, who were on the other side of the city. Plus it was dark by then. Already curfew. So there I was, alone, staring at the floor and feeling the walls shudder when Abdallah burst through the door. And behind Abdallah, calm as can be, Alessio. He had made his way across the entire city, the entire city through that inferno, at full speed, headlights off, so that I wouldn't be alone.

Here, in this same corner.

With that same poster in front of me, hanging crookedly.

Listening to the mortars.

I listen to the mortars as you listen to the sea from the shore, salt and time running through your fingers.

I listen to the mortars as though they were the most natural thing in the world to me.

A couple of them explode nearby. A little too close. I should move, I think, but what will that change? What difference will it make? No one will be coming through that door anymore.

Aleppo? What sense did it make to go back there again? that's how Lorenzo greeted me when I returned to Antakya. There's nothing to write about anymore. They are where they were a month ago.

"I left flowers for Abdallah."

He cut me short: "I don't want to get involved," he said. "Those are stories I don't want to get drawn into."

But we're all already drawn into them.

IN HIS OWN way, Assad was right. He told us Syria is different.

Because the Arab Spring was essentially a revolt against regimes that were more focused on the interests of the few in command, and on their Western friends, than on the interests of their own citizens. A revolt that succeeded only in Tunisia and Egypt, of course—the rest is something of a disaster, while at the same time marking the downfall of post-colonialism, of the old geography of formal sovereignties and extensive dependencies. It also swept away the theory that more than any other underpinned it. After the collapse of the Berlin Wall, in a world in which democracy, nation by nation, seemed to be catching on everywhere, the exception was the Middle East. Whose culture, it was argued, was not suited to democracy. It was the theory of Arab exception: a theory now disproved by a thousand Tahrir Squares and, first and foremost in fact, by years of social unrest and labor conflicts. The April 6 movement, an icon of resistance against Mubarak, is named in memory of April 6, 2008, when police fired at striking workers. The Arab Spring did not materialize from Facebook. And it was, essentially, a demand for self-determination. For substantive, not just formal, sovereignty.

For real power: the power to decide.

For all to decide: not just a privileged few. And to do so without external interference.

And it is in this sense that Syria is different and Assad was right. Because to make any predictions, do any analysis, it's pointless by now to look to Damascus. To question Assad and his objectives. Or the objectives of the opposition. As in the old Middle East, the war in Syria has now become a proxy war. Fought to advance the strategies of others.

Because it began as freedom against oppression. But it's

becoming Iran against Saudi Arabia, and therefore, they tell you, Sunni Islam against Shia Islam.

Because Syria, they say, isn't really that complicated.

"Trust me," one of the veteran journalists in Beirut reassured me, one of those who pay you $300 here, while you learn a little more about the craft. "It seems complicated," he said, "but in thirty years at the front, thirty years in the Middle East, in the end it was all about oil and Islam. Trust me."

Except that there are things you encounter just by taking a step back.

Meaning a step back from the front. Or more precisely, looking at what's around it.

Like Loubna Mrie. Not only is she an activist where everyone is supposed to be a terrorist. Not only is she a woman where there should only be men. But she is an Alawite, here where this war is supposed to be Sunnis against Shiites.

She is the one who continues Abdallah's work.

"The war is changing, it's true. But it is not true that we are Syrians against Syrians, Sunnis against Shiites. We are Syrians against Assad. Because even when we talk about Islam, we never talk only about Islam. Assad has Iran's support for Shiite solidarity, of course, but mainly because it is through Syrian territory that Hezbollah, in Lebanon, receives arms from Iran, and in the interests of Iran keeps pressure on Israel. Then too, in addition to Iran, Assad has Russia at his side, and Russia is not Shiite. But Russia has its last Mediterranean naval base in Syria, in Tartus, and only through Syria can it still have a say in the Middle East. And even more importantly than Tartus, Putin stands with Assad because he knows that every revolt for freedom, even the most distant, is a spark that can ignite Russia. As far as Putin is concerned,

no one should intervene in Syria because no one should intervene in Chechnya."

She looks younger than twenty-two. She has long, brown,
curly hair, gentle features, and a sweet gaze. You could meet
her outside of any high school: the same backpack, the same
striped shirt, the same dreams. She could be on her way to
march against cuts in education. Because Loubna has that
look: the intense gaze of certain sixteen-year-olds who stare
at you, unblinking. They seem fragile, but they're staring at
you because they won't budge.

She comes from Latakia, in Assad's home province. She
comes from a family of officers in the security forces. Like
her mother, Loubna immediately sided against the regime.
But for her and her mother, the regime coincided with the
male members of the family. They had been warned: another
demonstration, and you will be killed. And when, in August,
a video in which Loubna explained the objectives of the revolution ended up on YouTube, her mother disappeared. Executed. By men carrying out her father's orders.

Promises are kept.

"I cried for three days, devastated by feelings of guilt. Then
I thought: my mother would not want to see me here crying.
And I came back to gather medicine for Homs."

"No one called me. Not my grandmother, my aunts:
nobody. Not my friends. For fear of retaliation. That was the
worst part of it. The isolation. There I was leafing through
the phonebook, looking for someone to talk to, and—and
I had no one anymore. In Latakia they are all with Assad
because on television Assad repeats twenty times a day that
Syria is overrun with terrorists, Islamic fundamentalists paid
by the Israelis to cut our throats. He claims he's protecting the

minorities. Democracy. Yet he killed my mother. And he will kill me if he finds me. Here it doesn't matter if you are Christian, Sunni, Buddhist. The truth is that this regime, if you are against it, will kill you."

The Alawites, a Shiite minority to which the Assad family belongs, make up about 12 percent of the population. We don't know much about them, because they practice an esoteric cult, whose sacred texts are not public, and which are revealed only in part, and only to males. The cult is syncretic, with many elements of Christianity and Sunni Islam. For this reason they have long been stigmatized as heretics, and persecuted. Alawites, in Arabic, means "followers of Ali," the son of Muhammad: whom, in fact, the Alawites worship more than the Prophet.

"After September 11 everything came down to Islam. Economic, social, and political factors disappeared from any analysis of the Middle East: it all stemmed from religion. The Arab Spring was able to fracture the equation Arab equals Muslim. In Tunisia and Egypt they saw Tunisians and Egyptians, not Muslims and Christians. Here, however, everyone uses religion, the specter of a denominational war, for their own objectives—largely secular. But it makes no sense to define the regime as Shiite, even though the Assads are Shiite and the military leaders are Shiite: because state ownership of the means of production has enabled the Assads to create patronage networks that have benefited the middle class, which is predominantly Sunni. This is nothing but a regime of predators, and the opposition is composed entirely of the poor and the excluded. Shiites, Sunnis, and Christians alike. Everyone focuses on religion. But to understand Syria, Abdallah was right: Marx is more useful than the Koran."

So Assad was right. Syria is different.

There's only one point, I said to Abdallah, on which Syria does not appear to be different: Europe, as usual, is absent. The priority for us is the economy: save Greece, save Spain—but not Syria. And yet it emerged today that, during the war in Libya, France bought Gaddafi's satellite coordinates from Assad, in order to eliminate Gaddafi before he talked about his highly placed friends overseas. And paid for it with the pledge to keep silent.

The pledge not to intervene.

Syria really is different.

The only time when Europe clearly chose sides.

"BUT WHAT'S THE objective?" I ask, crawling into the kind of trench I've only seen in history books, the mud ankle-deep. They point to a kind of depository, two hundred yards ahead. A lopsided cement cube. "To capture that." "And what then?" I ask foolishly. "To capture that one," and they point to another depository, another cement box. Another three hundred yards farther on. "And then the one on the right": another twenty yards. All the way to Damascus, 250 miles.

The Aleppo airport is on the eastern edge of the city, and within it a military airport and Brigade 80, besieged by dozens of jihadists who came here to reinforce the revolution, arriving from Tunisia, from Libya, from Afghanistan, from Chechnya—and from various European outposts. On the fronts where Al Qaeda is fighting, the most commonly spoken language is not Arabic, it's English.

The battle began in December. Because it's from the airport that supplies travel to the section of Aleppo under the control of the regime and in particular to its soldiers; for the rebels, occupying the airport is critical. Because the idea, originally, was to advance from city to city. From north to south, map in hand: Idlib, Aleppo, Hama, Homs, Damascus. But after two years and eighty-five thousand deaths, we are still in Idlib. Still twenty-five miles from the Turkish border. And so the Islamists, more experienced, changed their strategy a day after they arrived. They don't advance from city to city anymore—those cities impossible to manage, because after all the fighting, the blood and rubble, the dead, in the end it's still the regime that governs half of it, while cold and hunger reign over the other half, along with Syrians who come to ask for bread. Instead the rebels advance from military base to military base. And this week they launched a decisive offensive—after the decisive offensive of three weeks ago.

Except that Assad's superiority lies in his air force, and planes don't take off from here. "Allah Akbar," Kadyr reassures me. God is great. "Anyway, we aren't here for this or that airport. We're here to testify that it is useless to oppose the will of the people," he explains. Even though Kadyr is Chechen. What does he know about the will of the people, if these aren't his people? "We are all men. All brothers," he snaps back. "But the Syrians want democracy," I say. "They want to decide their own future for themselves, don't they?" "Why, did you ask the Iraqis, the Afghans, before deciding their future? Those who are on the side of right win. Only God knows, Allah Akbar. God alone decides."

Kadyr is twenty-seven years old, a Chechen from Grozny, and he's here because Russia exterminated his family and supports Assad. Aazar is Afghani, thirty-one years old, and his father was killed by a mine, just like the daughter of Faryal, twenty-seven, also Afghani. It was a mine manufactured in Italy, he makes clear, and doesn't speak to me anymore. To his right is Ajeeb, twenty-three years old, Libyan. He lost his mother in an air strike; so did Masun, twenty-five years old, Iraqi, who is a carpenter with a degree in biology. Djamal, on the other hand, twenty-one years old, is from Marseilles, of Algerian origin. He is wearing a Zidane T-shirt and has "nothing to lose."

But this is not the best time for a sociological survey of Al Qaeda.

A mortar, to our right, hits the trench: and the fighting suddenly explodes around us. Because it's nothing but an earthen ditch we're in, hidden among the bushes and piles of bricks and stones and rusty iron. A vintage World War I trench, the kind that makes you think that Field Marshal Cadorna will soon appear with reinforcements on horseback. And three of the men simply disappear, pulverized. We have to move and fast, in the time it takes to reload. The mortar is fired from a semi-mobile position; a second strike always follows the first. We scuttle away like rats, heads down, the second shot striking even closer. We run faster. The only shelter is a concrete wall, but it's twenty yards away. And the trench is destroyed. While Aazar and Faryal cover us with a barrage of fire, we dash across one by one, flying through the bullets, minds switched off, the air now thick with dirt, dust and leaves, shards, unidentifiable fragments. Kadyr slips and is killed, the mortars keep coming, relentless. They're getting closer and closer. They'll reach us, Djamal screams, we're already dead: there's nothing left to do but attack.

Djamal is the first to bolt and head toward the depository, while I take shelter behind a half-charred passenger bus, an old advertisement still visible on its side: *Welcome to Syria*. Djamal is hit almost immediately; the sniper continues firing at him while the others, behind him, rush out all together and in a minute, in a second, it's war, war like in the movies, bodies running, falling—war that seems like madness, while Djamal, on the ground, goes on shooting until his last gasp. From the two rear zones facing us, RPGs are fired, rockets launched, while Kalashnikovs resound from within the depository. And at every death, the cry: "Allah Akbar." They drag me over to the bodies, pulpy masses of flesh and blood and agonized expressions that act as a barrier. Sometimes one of them seems to jerk. To move. But it must be a hallucination, because the battle goes on for two hours. The pile of corpses keeps growing and growing; the dead touch you, look at you, ooze onto you. Ajeeb makes an opening in the tangle of limbs, and shoots from there, coldly. Minute after minute, like a bottomless pit, for every body that comes back, another one rushes out, with only this cry, "Allah Akbar," Ajeeb makes a dash and sprints, swallowed up by the depository—until a mortar hits the right side, sweeping half of it away. That's when someone, from the trench, throws a firebomb. Smoke. Then something, inside, explodes. And all is lost, everything inside now silent.

"Allah Akbar, Allah Akbar," a Chechen keeps repeating. And he embraces Ajeeb.

"Allah Akbar, we won. We won."

As the flames devour everything, including his companions.

And while some, on the other side of the front, no doubt, are also contemplating the ashes, at this moment, and exulting: we won.

"DO YOU KNOW she's come from Syria?" one barista said to the other barista. "But you're not Syrian," the barista said to me. "No," I said. "I'm a journalist." "Oh," he said. "And you're in Syria?" "In Aleppo." "Oh. Aleppo." He said: "Awesome." Then: "I have a Tunisian friend, you know? He makes fabulous desserts. Absolutely fabulous," the barista said. "If you ask me, it's the flour." And the other barista added: "Sure." He said: "It's always the flour. What's the flour in Aleppo like?" he asked me. "Last time," I said, "last time it was flour made from leaves." "From leaves?" "Right. Leaves. Syria is a bit—has been struggling a bit in recent months. Having some problems." "Still," he said. "Flour made from leaves." Then he said to his friend: "Did you hear that? Leaves!" He said to me: "Do you have the recipe?"

The cappuccino in Livorno, at the café in the train station, was magnificent. I came back for a training session in HEAT, which would be Hostile Environment Awareness Training, an intensive course which is now required for war correspondents. Which doesn't exist in Italy, however, since foreign affairs in Italy are limited to attending Juventus's away games. And so the only course to attend is the one for officials of the European Union organized by the Scuola Superiore Sant'Anna of Pisa and the Carabinieri Corps of Tuscania, the special forces stationed in Livorno.

It's a training session in which you basically learn how to react in an ambush, or if you should step into a minefield. You learn to decipher a map. To communicate by satellite, to encrypt communications, stanch a severed vein, take cover from enemy fire, things like that. Like don't rattle your kidnappers. Because in war everything works ass-backwards. And whereas the last thing a normal person, so to speak, would think of doing when approaching a checkpoint is to switch off the headlights and arrive at the post with the headlights out (I don't know about you, but I'm from the South, and in Puglia only smugglers drive with their headlights off), here you have to drive up to a checkpoint with your headlights off and interior lights on, because that's the only way the guard on duty is able to see you and identify you. Well, to make a long story short, they teach you these kinds of things. Otherwise you'd act properly, turn on your headlights and fasten your seat belt, here in a war where everybody is armed, and they might mistake you for a smuggler at the first checkpoint and shoot you.

Because an entirely different logic applies in war. For example, the first lesson for soldiers is that it's better to wound than to kill. Because if you kill the enemy, he'll be left lying there and his comrades will go on fighting. But if you wound him, he'll start writhing, struggling for breath, and the whole unit will be out of action at that point because they'll have to help him. Everything about war is like that. Certain subtle lines of reasoning that you listen to admiringly, and then you think: we might use all this ingenuity in cancer research.

Well, anyway. For a week I'm here in Livorno with the Carabinieri.

Actually another reason I came back to Italy is because they finally figured out what the infection was, after I returned from Aleppo the last time, throwing up in the street every couple of yards and passing out in front of my door in Antakya. It was typhus. Despite being vaccinated and all. A particularly violent strain. And needless to say I'm very proud of my typhus. I nearly celebrated when the doctors pronounced it. I swear,

I would have made a toast, were it not that I felt nauseous just taking a sip of water. Because since I'm the only woman in Aleppo, the others with all their testosterone insisted that it was a psychological thing. While I lay there with a fever and cramps, they kept saying, no, it was all in my head, it was fear, it was because I was too fragile for war. And so, in front of the shocked doctors who'd confirmed that it was typhus, typhus! I called Lorenzo and with my last ounce of strength told him: "You see? I have typhus! I have typhus!" I chirped happily, before ending the call and passing out again. At which one doctor said to the other: "Still, I wouldn't rule out that it's psychological."

After being on a drip for a while, here I am, back again. Pretty emaciated but still standing.

Except that I'm in this weird course. I don't mean weird because of the Carabinieri— the Tuscania corps are "special" forces in the true sense of the word. They're stationed where the soldiers are but to apply the methods of a police force; that is, they're there to ensure order, not to demolish it—a difference which to soldiers, especially American soldiers, is not always clear. No, I mean weird because—take mortars, for example. With good reason, because it's a subject that particularly interests me. Gabriele, the captain, is very kind, and also very patient, since he has to explain it to me four times. What I want to know is: When the first one explodes, given that a second one is coming, where should I run? To the right, to the left? Straight ahead? Or maybe I should stay still. But stay still where? On the ground? Behind a wall? And Gabriele is very considerate. The mechanism, he says, is simple, it's like a range between two points. The first blow lands a little in front, the second a little behind. The third is the one meant to hit. And, I confess, I'm a little unclear on how to tell in front from behind. But most of all: "Hit what?" I ask him. He looks at me, puzzled. He says: "Hit the target."

So the mortar has a target then.

"Of course," he says. "It's not as if you fire at random."

Right. It's not as if you fire at random.

And then, things like the criteria for choosing a specific house. 1) Far away from the front. 2) If possible, not near sensitive targets such as a government office or barracks. 3) Preferably close to essential services. Like a market. Or a pharmacy. To avoid having to cross half the city at night in search of toothpaste. And my question is: "What about when essential services are sensitive targets?" "Well," Gabriele says, "then near the hospital." The hospital, he says, is always the safest bet.

The hospital. "And what if the hospital were, let's say, too far away? And there's shooting, everywhere. Where should I take cover? Given that the hospital—let's say you can't take shelter there."

"Well," Gabriele says, "then the refugees. You mix in with the refugees. They can't very well fire at the refugees," he says.

Of course.

The refugees.

They can't very well fire at the refugees.

War has its rules. Its manuals.

It's not as if you fire at random.

And so in the evening I study. Or at least I try to. For instance, I study how a satellite phone works. Then I remember Marie Colvin, a correspondent for the *Sunday Times*, killed in Homs, and I think that with a satellite phone they can pinpoint you, in Syria, and drop a mortar on your head. So I switch to another chapter. I look for the chapter on snipers. Because that subject, too, is of particular interest to me. But there isn't one, there's no chapter on snipers because if a sniper hits you, you're dead, even with the best flak jacket. And so there's no chapter on snipers. Next I study how to recognize a rebel. A rebel a) is positioned in a chain of command, b) has a visible weapon, c) is wearing a distinguishing badge, d) — d) I think the most distinctive thing I've seen, in Syria, to be able to tell if someone is a rebel, are the flip-flops. And so every evening I end up trying to study, but then I close the book and read something else. Because they are always so reassuring, these manuals. And like the international law manuals, there are civilians and combatants, and there is a front, always; there's a here and a there, and there are also journalists, with their press badge. There's never anyone in these manuals who has been incinerated by a missile that he didn't hear coming.

Meanwhile there's a knock at the door. I put the book down and open up.

It's Ronan, one of two Irish members of the special forces. They're here as instructors of a similar course. The two of them are really proficient, with years of experience all over the world; watching them in action is like being at the movies. We have supper together, usually. They're intrigued by Syria, and more interested in Syrians suffering through the war than in those fighting it. And so we meet for supper.

"In the spring we'd like to have you in Dublin," Ronan tells me. "A conference. It would be interesting if you were to come and tell us how things are in Syria."

"You could tell us how the war is changing," he adds.

We lie under the network of arching shells and live in a suspense of uncertainty. Over us, Chance hovers. If a shot comes, we can duck, that is all; we neither know nor can determine where it will fall. [. . .] It is just as much a matter of chance that I am still alive as that I might have been hit. In a bomb-proof dug-out I may be smashed to atoms and in the open may survive ten hours' bombardment unscathed. No soldier outlives a thousand chances. But every soldier believes in Chance and trusts his luck.

It's 1918 in the book I'm reading: *All Quiet on the Western Front.**

---

* Erich Maria Remarque, *All Quiet on the Western Front*, trans. A. W. Wheen (New York: Fawcett Books, 1982), 101.

April is April even in Syria, sprightly, its hills newly speckled, all primroses and violets, the white flowering boughs of almond, the orange of the tulips, and this mild, gentle wind, laden with sunlight and jasmine. By contrast, in the house to your left, yesterday—it was nearly evening—Asma committed suicide. A bullet to the head. April isn't April in Syria. She was thirteen years old.

The province of Idlib, in the north, borders on Turkey, and was the first to be captured by the rebels who have their bases in Turkey. But a "liberated area," here, is by no means a safe zone. Because this is the land of missiles: every day they drop down on you, randomly, unexpectedly. The rebels still have no anti-aircraft protection other than bad weather and haze. Missiles and Islamists. They come from Libya, from Tunisia, from Afghanistan, veterans of a thousand other wars; without them the regime would already have suppressed every revolt. No one knows what their objectives really are. They are feared and invisible. Few Kalashnikovs around, few checkpoints. Life seems to go on as usual, but everything is chaos, everything unreadable. It's a dry wind that blows, sun-drenched and thick with fear.

Jabal al-Zawiya is a nature reserve studded with Roman and Byzantine tombs, stretches of meadow among pale, barren rocks. But then you spot a glitter, under a stone arch, in shadow, hidden among the bushes, and it's the metal of a teapot. Between a book lying sodden in the grass, a torn strip of a shirt, you see a silvery reflection. And it's not one of the many rocks, but a plastic tarp.

It's a door.

They emerge from underground, dozens of them. Gaunt, barefoot, looking haggard and tattered. They took refuge here, to await the end of the war in this damp, fetid air, the vaults of the crypts blackened by the carbon of wood-burning stoves. They sleep on the sepulchers. And they cough, they cough continuously from tuberculosis, like Nader Khaled al-Badwy, twenty-six, and his wife Sanaa, twenty-two, nineteen-month-old Omar in her arms. Nader turns a box of medicine around in his hands: it's the only thing he found in the pharmacy, the instruction sheet is in English. "Better than nothing," he says. It's medicine for meningitis. All they have is bread and tea, rainwater to drink. Another child, seven months old, is in Turkey; every so often they try to send her a bottle of mother's milk through a smuggler. They've been here since September, and since September not a soul has passed through. Not an NGO, not the Red Cross. Not a single doctor without borders. No one. They've received no aid whatsoever. Nor do they have the slightest expectation, by now. I ask them about the National Coalition, the organization of opposition forces based in Istanbul, which recently appointed a prime minister and a provisional government. What would they ask the Coalition for, if they could? Their only response is: sugar.

The hills look the same as always in Syria, but then you notice these tall, scrawny trees, looking like spikes stuck in the ground, spaced apart from each other, these strange trees, and you don't get it. These spikes. Then you realize that they are just tree trunks, their branches missing. To keep warm, people here sawed off the branches. One by one. "But not the trees. This is a protected park."

They live crowded together, twenty-two of them, in these two underground tombs. The youngest is called Malaki, she's two months old, and you can barely see her in her cradle amid the flies. They are the families of Ahmad Omar al-Yahya, forty-five, and Basam al-Amnou, forty-two. They buried everything under an olive tree. And they moved in here, ducking their heads, the vaults too low, a cigarette lighter for illumination, the only latrine marked not so much by a wall of bricks and the ooze of sewage, as by a swarm of insects. Beetle casings, and when it rains, the tombs get flooded so they stay outside. Out in the rain. One little boy has a bruised face, a broken wrist, because they slither in through steep passages, muddy tunnels, and he slipped a week ago. Their homes, in nearby al-Bara, were swept away by an air strike, eleven families pulverized. As of today, 6 missiles and 275 mortars have hit al-Bara, population 5,000. The one we hear now is number 276. A mortar, we say, then we go on talking.

Refugees of the Syrian War—which as of March 15 had been going on for two years—number more than a million. But the UN's statistics refer to evacuees in the camps set up in Jordan, Lebanon, Turkey, and Iraq. They don't record the IDPs (internally displaced persons) who have remained here. Who are estimated to be four million, and who have nothing. Nothing. The international NGOs are still settling in, still at the border, engaged in yet another assessment and planning meeting, while the local ones are often nothing more than impromptu acronyms of Syrians who have returned after years abroad to pocket donations. And the UN, by statute, operates through the Damascus government, with the result that aid is distributed in areas under the control of the regime. "But to get to Turkey is costly . . ." Mariam al-Mohamad, fifty-seven, explains, interrupted by another explosion. "It's partly that we're afraid of looting, and we don't want to leave. But it's also true that a car to the border costs $300, and three cars would be needed for an average family. Almost a year's salary. The truth is that to become refugees is a luxury we cannot afford."

Ahmad Haj Hammoud is thirty-one years old, and every day at 8 a.m. on the dot he clocks in to work in Idlib. He's a public employee there. Only the province is actually under rebel control. Everything in the city functions as usual, shops, offices. Schools. And there are many like Ahmad: part of the regime by day, its victims by night. "But I need the money," he says briefly. "And I just want this war to end." A great many in Syria are neither with Assad nor with the rebels. They're simply tired. Caught between a vicious regime and the opposition: disorganized twenty-year-olds with T-shirts and rifles. "Not only don't they have any plan for the future. The problem is that they don't even have rules for the present. They only think about themselves. They confiscated the granaries, the flour, and left everyone to starve, saying that the front took priority. That they need energy to win. To liberate us. But to be liberated, we must be alive."

Another explosion meanwhile. They're fighting a few miles from here in Maraat al-Numan. It's right above Aleppo-Damascus. Strategic for a southward advance. The name Maraat

al-Numan is a graft of the Greek name Arra, the Christian
name Marre, and the location's first Muslim ruler, an-Numan
ibn Bashir. "A synthesis of the Syria of old, in which we all
lived together," says Habib al-Hallaq, twenty-six, a Sunni
deserter who in Damascus had a house in an Alawite district.
"A synthesis of today's Syria," Noura Nassouh, forty-seven,
his neighbor in the tomb, corrects him. "In which we are all
killed, without distinction."

Because April isn't April in Syria, and in this illusory spring
studded with buds and mortars, this is how they live, on
bread and tea and rainwater. What seems like silver is instead
plastic. What seems like stillness, is death. They are workers,
a greengrocer, a house painter, a policeman, but also biolo-
gists and engineers, dropped here with a degree, a doctorate,
exhausted, in this life in the wild, waiting for it to be over,
wrapped up like beggars in whatever they've been able to
find, hair like stubble, that drained, haggard expression and
eyes like ashes. On their cell phones, beautiful photographs
of Aleppo, of Damascus, of homes with pastel painted tiles,
wrought iron lamps. They talk in choppy phrases, head down,
while with their bare hands they try to shape a sheet of metal
into a tray and cut themselves. A trickle of blood barely oozes
its way through the scabs, calluses, and blisters on their fingers. All they'll say is: "I had a life like yours once. Ray-Bans
just like yours."

Suad is fifteen days old and her eyes are already red and
wrinkly; she was born here, in a tomb, in a dawn of missiles.
Her mother's name is Adlalh Ziady, she's nineteen years
old and stares at me in silence, her skin sallow. Meanwhile
a mortar explodes, someone dies, and while I think about
what to ask her, she goes on staring at me in silence. While

I think: What does it feel like, to give birth in a tomb? Are you afraid? Uncertain? And when this revolution started, when the demonstrations started, did you imagine it would be like this? While she goes on staring at me in silence, not a word. And I keep thinking, as another mortar explodes: Did they bomb your house? And where were you? I think, and how does it feel when they bomb your house? And foolishly: What do you need most urgently, milk? medicine? The sting of shame, when you come out of the tomb, children have picked all those flowers for you, and cling to your arm, as if you were worthy, as if you were here to save them, and instead they don't know, with their flowers, they don't know, we're only here for another article that won't seduce any consciences, not even our own, as they cling to your arm and don't know, they don't know that they don't matter, because what is there to understand, still, in Syria, what is there to ask? While Adlalh stares at me in utter silence and doesn't speak. And rightly so, because she has nothing to say, as another mortar explodes and a woman hunched in the corner, her fifty years seeming more like seventy, three children dead, not even a body remaining, covers her face with her hands, motionless, and she too is silent. If the Syrians have ended up in crypts, Syrian women have ended up huddled in the corners.

It's *Spoon River* in reverse, this life in which the living, from their tombs, talk to the dead, who watch and don't hear. Amen al-Yassin is thirty-seven years old, and together with his wife, his mother, and eleven children, the youngest five months old, lives in a stable, among goats and chickens. On a shelf are grimy jars of olives and spices, a sack of potatoes, moldy bread, that's all; hanging from a dog chain, there's laundry so tattered that you can't say if something is a shirt or a sweater, or what color it is. Their house, in Kafr Kouma, is in ruins, and they haven't found another place. For this stable, which can be hit by a missile at any time, just like their old house, they pay 5,000 lire per month, compared to the 4,000 lire they paid in rent before—but for a real house. Because only in novels do war and poverty inspire solidarity: in real life they breed speculation, borders populated with traffickers and wheeler-dealers. You pay for everything here, for a car to Turkey, for a bottle of mother's milk. To sleep in a chicken coop. And you pay three times the normal rate. Another mortar. "I'm looking for a tomb. But they're all occupied now. And the remaining ones, on private lands, are even more expensive."

Ismail Khodor al-Yosef is seventy-five years old; his heart is failing following a myocardial infarction, his bones sculpt his skin like a bas-relief, and he is lying on the ground waiting to die. His wheezing gasps pierce the thick air of early afternoon like broken bottle shards. It is not one of those deaths that you get used to in war: abrupt, terse, a bullet and you're gone, no—it's a harsh, protracted death, agonizing, the death of a man clinging to life, his eyes doggedly fixed on the light. He was the park's watchman. He has no word of his children, all of them refugees. And lying on the ground, his wife behind him like a Pietà who will never have her Michelangelo, he stares solely at the light, in the tomb of a man whose name nobody knows, as he too slowly, simply, passes on.

ALEPPO IS STARVING, stricken by a typhus epidemic, people are selling everything they own in the streets. It seems like everyone has emptied his living room: teapots, TVs, telephones, tablecloths, light switches, anything and

everything—or more precisely, bits and pieces of anything
and everything. Because Aleppo is nothing but rubble, so
someone sells you a stroller, another the wheels. Ibtisam
Ramdan, twenty-five years old, lives with tuberculosis and
three children in a section of drainage pipe below the riverbank, with chicken coop mesh for a door, a paint drum
for a stove, and those three children crying and coughing
in a dark, dank corner, coughing so hard and crying so
desperately that they gasp for breath. On a scrap of cardboard, the remains of rice. They don't have dishes, and in
any case, there's nothing edible around here right now. And
like them, dozens of others. The entire riverbank is riddled
with clefts and hollows; they aren't shacks, they aren't caves,
they're nothing but pieces of things—sheet metal, wooden
planks, plastic tarps—aggregations of pieces of things. At
some point you're simply inside, among women, children,
old people maimed and speechless, those toothless mouths.
You pass an inch from them and they don't even look at
you, faces blackened from the coal stoves, skin covered with
infections. Even the cats are sick. A plane roars above and
in your head. You try to push open a door and discover a
man dying of leukemia; you try another one and find a man
skinning a rat; then another door to find only this girl: blank,
motionless as if absent. You attempt to ask a question, and
your interpreter breaks down in tears and says, "I'm sorry,
but I have no more words, I have no more words for all this."

Aleppo is starving, so devastated that the missiles strike,
and people stay put and live among the rubble. Like in Ard
al-Hamra, 117 dead, 17 of whom are still under there, scattered
beneath you. The living emerge before you, one by one, from
staircases, collapsed ceilings, caved-in floors, stumps of sup-

porting columns, a carpet hanging from the blades of a fan. All they have is what they have with them. Fouad Zytoon, thirty-six, shows you a photo on his Nokia: the head pitched on a shelf is his daughter. They insist on telling you all the details. "Do you want the names of the victims?" they ask you, "I have the full list," and you're ashamed to say it, but no, you don't need the names, just the total number, besides it's late, and Aleppo is a thousand stories and this is only one line of your article; it's late, really, and besides you're tired, and dusty, and you're terrified by the aircraft over your head, which keeps circling and circling and circling, the pilot deciding whom to bomb, maybe he's choosing you, so no, all you need is the number, thanks, that's all: 117, seventeen of whom were not recovered. And the young man looks at you, point-blank, and says, "You see? There's nothing left of our lives, not even a name."

Aleppo seems normal. And the journalists are gone. Grass has grown among the ruins, the war has become the city's face. Taxi drivers see you with the Nikon around your neck, and they stop you, as if you're a tourist. They ask you: "Want to go to the front?" But then you run into a little girl, smiling, blond, and she snaps to attention and gives the military salute. Then you come across a street cleaner and an electrician repairing an antenna, and suddenly, like the crack of a whip, their bodies drop. Hit by a sniper. Then as the plane appears, disappears, reappears, levels out, climbs again, unidentified dead bodies lie at the entrance to the hospital and people pass by, lift the sheet slightly, make sure it's not a brother, a cousin. Then you go into a playground, while maybe the pilot is choosing you, while maybe it's your turn, and among the swings there's a sleeping bag, and inside the sleeping bag there's a boy who is purplish, a hole in his temple, and while these are the cruelest

moments, you look around, and everywhere around you, devastated by artillery, there are only houses with one floor inhab-
ited, another floor mangled, a charred tricycle hanging in
mid-air, in the wind, waiting, a lamp, a curtain swaying, fossil
remains of normal lives. Because Aleppo seems normal, but
then you walk into a school, a classroom, children bent over
their books in silence, and the teacher shows you their draw-
ings—"My best friend"—and one is a child amid the rubble,
another a child missing a leg, one is a sheet of paper, red, all
red, a sheet sodden with blood, while maybe it's your turn,
now, and all you can do is huddle there, along with everything
you've left unsaid in your life, the times you weren't capable
of loving, the times you weren't capable of risking, the words
that remained caught in your fingers, the times that . . . now
it's too late though, it's too late for everything, and life holds a
fierce beauty now that maybe it's your turn.

Until excitedly, then, a man comes, and announces: Sheik
Said has been bombed. And it's tasteless to admit it, but—it's
hard, but it's an infinite relief. Sheik Said: not you. An infinite
relief. Knowing that someone is dead. And it's as if this war
has robbed you not of humanity, but has suddenly and still
more violently, as if—as if—as if it's left you naked in front
of the mirror, exposed for what you really are, because you're
all that matters in your life, it bleeds to admit it, but this war
hasn't robbed you of anything, of anything, your humanity,
your diverse selves, simply—never existed. All that matters is
you. And what kind of a life is a life like that?

The reporters have gone away, one by one. Yes, Aleppo
seems normal. The front, however, is still here. You know
you're close to it when a procession of Syrians fleeing in the
opposite direction to yours begins. Dozens of vehicles pro-

filed against a sky seething with explosions, vans loaded with everything you can think of: it's not exactly the image you'd associate with "liberation." The refugees take everything with them, refrigerators, sofas, even potted plants, because otherwise it will all be stolen. The rebels empty out the shops. They strip the machinery in the factories. They sell the marbles, the inlaid wood window frames. They sell the blankets, the carpets. The dishes. Everything. That's how the front advances, city to city, district to district; it advances like a tsunami, and in its wake nothing is left, only children playing ball in the dust. The regime bombs everything that's bombable, and the rebels drive around in their jeeps to arrest, torture, and sometimes execute on the spot anyone suspected of collusion with the regime—or anything—at their discretion.

Shabia.

After the fighting, the bombings, it's always this way. After the bombings, the looting. And after the looting, feuding among the rebels for control of the ruins. "It's all just stories made up by the journalists!" their spokesman challenges me as we make our way through a market. Meanwhile, he buys some rice clearly labeled: "Aid. Not for sale."

Even humanitarian aid is resold here.

The Syrians are resolutely against the regime, but also, and increasingly, against the rebels accused of having dragged Aleppo into a war they were never prepared to fight, with their tuna can grenades. And now accused of looting and extortion as well, and in particular of having handed the country over to Jabhat al-Nusra. To Al Qaeda's men.

They came here from Sudan, from Somalia, from the United States. From Belgium. From Bosnia and Sweden. From Yemen. From Indonesia, Ireland, and Romania. With their experience, with their sophisticated weapons, they altered the balance of the war and prevented a defeat that seemed certain. But they also altered the balance of Syria, a secular country. In support of Islam.

They continue to be a minority, according to estimates. They continue to make up about 5 percent of the rebels. But they also continue to be the most highly trained, the most well equipped: the ones who decide. And most importantly of all, they continue to be inaccessible. Not much is known about them. They don't speak to journalists. They run things by means of fatwas posted on the Internet. No one knows who issues them, and in the name of what authority. But it's well known how they're carried out. Because every so often you'll be walking in Aleppo, and you'll see a black jeep standing at the curb. Armored. The windows dark. And then a man. You see this man in front of you suddenly grabbed from behind, hit in the head. Thrown into the jeep. And to this day no one has ever returned to tell what happens next.

And not much more is known about them.

"But don't write that we are not democratic," a Saudi in their headquarters warns me. "If you have questions, you can find everything on our Facebook page."

The only certainty is that the Islamists don't have anti-aircraft protection either.

To reassure us, they stand there with their Dushkas, the slings pulled back, pointing toward the sky. But the only anti-aircraft is rain clouds. As Wael says: "The only refuge is luck." He's eight years old. And he goes back to playing ball, while every so often something around him explodes. Explodes and topples.

The Syrians stare at you, dazed, standing at the roadside like a tableau of Armageddon. But then a bus passes, and in that instant you think: like that one, that time, the one we hid behind, that time when there were snipers everywhere, and grenades. That bus: and that little boy, who had almost made it there, he too almost safe—but it's only an instant. And you keep moving. Only you duck into a house. Any house. And to the right, in the shadows, to the right there's a basement. A basement like that one—they were bombing, remember? They were bombing everything, and that man, when he gave you his place so you could stay alive and tell the world. Remember? When he said to you: "Your life is more important than mine." And then at the corner of al-Shifa. The asphalt barely buckled. But there were two craters, two bombs—where Alessio nearly died, where Narciso nearly died, and that wall in front—there was a corpse there, and a mortar—remember? A mortar that struck it dead-on, that disintegrated it, can't you hear it? There's a dead body in the air and at every corner, every corner. You walk along and try to keep moving, but at every corner, every corner of the entire city, there's another city behind the city, an echo behind every voice, a corpse behind every living being and this dust, these ashes, this memorial to an unknown civilian, when suddenly a child appears and clings to your arm and screams, "I've lost them all!" He screams it out, "I've lost them all!" and he tugs at you, and screams, and begs you, "I've lost them all." There, where a hand emerged once, and you feel like you're falling, while everything around you, suddenly, everything in front of you is a blur, fading in and out. "I've lost them all!" And he won't go away, he won't go away, he clings to you, "I've lost them all!" There, remember? There, where a head surfaced, where you thought they were flakes of plaster but they were slivers of human skull. There, the last time you saw Abdallah, can't you hear it? The first time you said I love you.

Until, exhausted, now gray with dust, you crawl out from among the usual sandbags to dodge yet another sniper. "How long before we get there?" you ask, nerves shattered. "Is it still far?" And it's only then that you understand this war: when you're in the middle of nowhere, and Alaa tells you: "We're already here."

Because all that remains of Aleppo's ancient souk, the bazaar—the most enchanting place, the iconic picture post-card of Syria with its tumult of voices, its stories and colors, the flurry of life—all that remains is this: rubble. Your feet sink up to your ankles in twisted spikes of rusty iron, glass, metal. The shutters are ripped open and riddled with bullets. Dust and stones. Nothing more. Truly nothing more. The rebels lead you from aisle to aisle, shop to shop. "This is the cotton market," they explain. "This is the goldsmiths' market, to the right are spices, back there silver." But the bazaar is nothing but rubble. "This is where brides come to buy their wedding dresses," and they point to a remnant of structure, "here their rings." Verbs in the present indicative: and all you see is . . . nothing. Here not even a mouse is stirring.

Iyad is thirty-two years old and has a fragile look despite his bulky muscles; he's a carpenter. "My workshop is the one in the corner," he says, even though there's only a collapsed ceiling and the remains of a wall in the corner, and even though he now works as a sniper, two hours a day, every day. He sleeps here, a mattress and a blanket beside the skeleton of a door. His brother is dead, his father is dead, his best friend is dead, everyone is dead, his two-year-old daughter is dead, a photo of her body lying in blood on his cell phone, and now he's a sniper, simply that, two hours a day behind a barrier of sand bags; you look through the opening from which he shoots and the helmets of the last soldiers he hit are still there, in the middle of the street. Any question you ask, Iyad has the same answer. "How does it feel the first time?" you ask him, and he shows you his daughter's body. "What goes through your mind as a man lies gasping in your viewfinder?" and he shows you his daughter's body. You ask him: "When all this is over, what will you do? And what will Syria be like?" and there's only his daughter's body, only the blood. Until he says: "Anything else you want to know?" puts the phone in his pocket, and goes back to shooting.

They're seventeen, eighteen, twenty years old, with those transparent eyes that you can look through to see the devastation behind them. They've been fighting here for months; the clock on the wall is stopped at 5:47 p.m. It was September 25, and Aleppo was an inferno, an explosion every few seconds, when the old city, a UNESCO Cultural Heritage of Humanity site, was engulfed in flames. They roam through the remains of the disaster with their Kalashnikovs, wearing T-shirts and Simpsons socks under their boots. They are the new masters of Aleppo, young kids who scarcely have diplomas, scarcely trades—but they have Kalashnikovs. They've gotten a whiff of power at this point and they won't go back to being nobodies, as they were in the old days of Assad. They've set up camp here with their portable stoves and sleeping bags, as if they were visiting on an InterRail pass. Talking to them is useless, you hardly get a word, hardly any reaction. They control every corner. Every vestige of wall has its checkpoint, its guards. They patrol the streets of an imaginary city. "This is the best tailor shop in Aleppo," and there's nothing there but a pile of jagged sheet metal that's under sniper fire.

And since you know Aleppo, when you come across a swarm of insects on a street corner like this, you know there are human remains under the pile.

And at some point, in a burst of mortar, something golden still glints. It's a chandelier. Curious, you duck your head, squeeze between the sandbags, wriggle inside, and you find yourself among dozens of copies of the Koran, all riddled with bullets: it's the old mosque.

What's left of it.

The walls defaced by artillery fire, the candelabra trashed. Engravings and decorations razed, the shades of red on the carpet now tinged with blood. And hung between the pillars, dark plastic sheeting: Assad's snipers are on the other side of the courtyard. Because Aleppo's war is a war of the past century; it's trench warfare. Rebels and loyalists are so close they shout insults at one another as they shoot. Your first time at the front, you can't believe it: bayonets you've only seen in history books, which you thought hadn't been used since Napoleon's reign. Now war is waged with drones; only here it's fought inch by inch, with a blade strapped to the barrel, rusted with blood, because it's a street-to-street battle, hand-to-hand combat, with stray dogs outside scuffling over a human bone. These young men are praetorians of an empire of death; they salute you with the victory sign as if they were posed in front of the Coliseum for a souvenir photograph, but all they stand before are demolished minarets, tangles of sheet metal. Then they stop the photographer: "Here, it is forbidden to enter," they say. "The area beyond is reserved for women." They stand guard over a hallucination, over the charred remains of things beyond recognition, among the ghosts of brides—here, where everything is more sacred than life.

It's like the blasted landscape in Cormac McCarthy's *The Road*. The muezzin doesn't even summon people to prayer. He's out looking for blood donors for victims injured by the last missile. Only a hail of Kalashnikovs jolts you awake when they start shooting again outside. It's the only sign of life. Out there, some are still alive. Some haven't yet died.

IN THE THRONGED alleyways of Bustan al-Qasr, one of Aleppo's poorest neighborhoods, they have to point him out to you three times. You would never recognize him, here in the crowd, even with a photograph of him in hand. He looks like any other Syrian: black hair, black eyes, and mustache. Small. He's thirty years old. In his white shirt, he has the ordinary look of a provincial clerk of the seventies.

But it's not his appearance that makes Abu Maryam a portrayal of Syrians today. Persecuted by the regime, he was then assaulted by the rebels. And is now wanted by the Islamists.

"I was cooking one evening in the mess hall, the canteen for displaced people, when I heard shots against a roll-up shutter. It was the Fatah brigade, trying to break into the warehouse on the corner. I went over and they said: 'It belongs to a *shabia*.' They said: 'We have orders to confiscate everything.' But we all know each other here, and it's not true, the owner is not a *shabia*. So I protested. But they surrounded me. Insulted me, shoved me. And at some point the butt of a rifle split my head open. And someone, while he was at it, stole my wallet."

Head trauma and thirteen stitches. "I honestly don't know who these guys are. Where they came from. Some of them are familiar faces: they took part in the demonstrations. With helmets and clubs. They were policemen. Those in the Free Army seem to be faithful to an old Arab proverb that says better the dog that barks with you than the dog that barks at you.

"And so the Islamists, at the beginning, in a situation like this, with all these guys out of control, these Kalashnikovs, the Islamists were a reliable presence. Correct, rigorous. Uncompromising. They not only stopped Assad, but also restored a minimum of public order. But then they started to show up at the demonstrations, demanding to replace our banners with theirs, which called for a caliphate instead of a democracy. They've never been loved here because, in the end, ours is a secular country, and even the Muslims have always distinguished between the private sphere and the political sphere. Still, the Islamists were respected. Today they are mainly feared. Whatever you say, they accuse you of being blasphemous. You tell them that weapons are prohibited at assemblies—you tell them to leave them outside—and they say you've offended the Prophet. You tell them that bread should be distributed here, not in the mosque, and they say you've offended the Prophet. One Friday, at a rally, I snatched their banners. The first time I escaped, the second time they arrested me. And whipped me."

He looks at me, he says, "I'm worried. They treat those who don't share their views the same way they treat criminals. That's what a regime does."

Abu Maryam, in fact, is not a Syrian like the others. He's the leader of Bustan al-Qasr, one of the most dangerous neighborhoods in Aleppo. The front winds in and out: sometimes you're walking along and you run into a barricade of tires and trash bins. It means they're shooting on the other side. On this side, those bins are the posts for a makeshift soccer field. Bustan al-Qasr is a kind of city within a city.

Its citizens are self-governing. They have their own schools, their own clinic. A radio station. They manage water, electricity. The canteen for displaced persons. The original plan developed by the Local Coordination Committees (LCCs), a pivotal force in Syria before the Free Army was formed, was to oust the regime not by destroying everything but by appropriating the institutions and reestablishing them with new people, new ideas. New practices. To renounce the officials of Ba'ath, the single party in which power in effect resided, ignore the laws, the orders, and adopt new ones. To reject the administrators appointed by the regime and elect new ones. Their own. "Without challenging Assad on the field that suits him most," said Abu Maryam: "the field of violence."

"Because with weapons it is obvious that he will win," he says. "But with numbers, we can choose. We can be bullets against air power. Or 22 million against one."

In theory, the Local Coordination Committees still exist.

Not only here. Throughout Syria.

But they never end up in the newspapers.

"I understand," Abu Maryam says. "I realize that Syria is one war among many, for you. That it's a bidding war. And that the mother who loses two children and reacts by shooting is more spectacular than one who reacts by adopting two orphans." I understand, he says. "The problem is that if you only talk about those who fight, any revolution becomes a war.

"The problem," he says, "is that my freedom depends on you as well."

Because it's true that even after 94,000 have died, after 1,663,713 have fled the country as refugees, the activists have not lost their energy. Their determination. After two years

and four months, only one thing has changed: now the protests are no longer just against Assad.

"I know that for you I am a symbol of today's Syria. Hunted
by everyone. By the regime, by the rebels, by the Islamists.
The perfect figure. But I am a symbol in another sense: I am
a symbol because I am still here. The rebels, the Islamists,
any of them can try to impose whatever they want. We are
no longer willing to obey. To submit. And that's an important
difference. It's the certainty that we will never go back. It's in
that sense that I am a symbol of today's Syria."

"Think of Hama," he says. "You can't understand today's
Syria unless you think of Hama."

Syrians in Hama, in fact, have always referred to what
occurred there simply as "Hama," without further specifica-
tion. "What happened in Hama." The fear, the terror, was so
great under the regime that Syrians never said the words "the
Hama massacre."

And yet, in twenty days, twenty thousand people were
killed. February 1982. That's how Hafez, Bashar's father,
squelched the revolt of the Muslim Brotherhood, which,
inspired by the Islamic Revolution in Iran in 1979, had tried
to overthrow the regime. Not only because it was a secular
regime, and governed by an Alawite moreover, but because
it was a regime aligned with the Soviet Union, explains Abu
Maryam. That is, a regime that steered the economy through
state-controlled five-year plans. Expropriations. Whereas the
Muslim Brotherhood was an expression of the bourgeoisie, of
an entrepreneurial class. As usual, to understand Syria, Marx
can be more useful than the Koran. In February 1982, three
years of clashes ended with the Hama massacre. The breeding
ground of the revolt.

The city was literally razed to the ground.

Annihilated.

And that's why so many here still believe that Assad can remain in power. Because what to us foreigners seems impossible after so much violence has already proved to be possible.

Yet that's why others believe the opposite.

Because Syria is complicated.

And so, those who think the opposite say these kids are our hope.

They are no longer willing to remain silent. To submit.

They insist that now that they've known freedom, they won't forget it.

The demonstrators gather every Friday, no exception, at the mosque.

Those who make up the procession that winds through the narrowest passageways to avoid being hit by mortars are seventeen, eighteen, twenty years old, no older than that. Adults at windows watch from the shadows. When the young people catch a glimpse of them, behind the slightly parted curtains, they yell from below: "Accomplices! Accomplices! Your silence is the voice of Assad!" And it's all that's left of the revolution. This handful of kids, nearly barefoot, scourged by starvation and typhus. Crutches, bandages. The van with the megaphone and amplifiers is still without fuel, still pushed by hand, while a young woman, in a bluesy voice, intones a poem in memory of the martyrs: "*Now that there's nothing left,*" she sings, "*now that there's nothing left of you but dust and tears,*" she sings as we wind slowly, cautiously, tensely expecting the first sniper around every curve and—and yet they sing, these kids, they go on singing, so vulnerable, their number swelling every few yards. Around every curve. And exposed like that, without gasoline, even then, as they beat the drums, the war in Syria suddenly seems to return to the Syrian Spring: no more missiles and bloodshed, no more rubble, only passion, again, only fervor and courage as the dancing begins, and as the young woman goes on singing, *"Now that you're gone, now that everything speaks to me of you,"* now as the surge, from the front row, widens, expands, swells and churns, and as you look at them, one by one, you who are of the same generation yet so different, so detached, how can you not feel drawn in? *"Now that I've lost you,"* how can you not feel swept away *"now that,"* she sings, *"what's left of you is me,"* as you look at them, you look at them and envy them, so strong, they're dancing, dancing and laughing, so strong, even then, even among the ghosts, even amid the ruins, while unlike them you weren't capable of feeling, in life, and . . .

And a mortar explodes.

On a building that has already been destroyed, actually. Three hundred yards away.

Maybe more. But the procession, instantly, scatters.

The asphalt remains littered with flip-flops, flags, bottles.

The megaphone. An overturned chair. A white one.

And only this van, sideways, in the deserted street. The music still playing.

The dust, slowly settling.

The place we've dashed into is a small shop, selling canned meat, mango juice. Stale biscuits. The owner is a tall young man. Thin. And he's just returned from his combat shift; like many he spends eight hours at the front, eight hours behind the counter. He notices the Nikon. "My wife is in the Free Army," he says. Ever since the story of Guevara went around the world, everywhere you turn here someone stops you to say: "My wife is in the Free Army." He says: "$100."

They live upstairs.

He's thirty-eight years old, she's twenty-six. She opens the door in jeans, but in a minute reappears in camouflage and a baseball cap with the Jabhat al-Nusra logo. Of their three children, the youngest is four months old and her name is Revolution. Her grandmother takes care of the baby, while she and her husband alternate between the front and the shop. Even though, at the front, she doesn't fight. She cooks. She primps for the photo, combs her hair, reapplies her makeup, eyebrow pencil. Revolution in one arm, a Beretta in the other hand.

Mahmoud, five years old, toddles in. A Pokémon T-shirt and a plastic gun. He comes in and tells me: "When I'm big I'm going to kill Assad." And then? Meaning, after you've killed Assad. What will you do then? Be a doctor? Or maybe an astronaut. You could be an astronaut, a soccer player. A violinist. Killing Assad isn't a profession. "I want to cut the infidels' throats," he says. "There are a lot of them," he says. "It won't take just one day."

Children.

Now that they've come to know war.

ALL I REMEMBER is the asphalt.

All of a sudden.

Which by then wasn't even asphalt anymore, covered by a kind of gravel made of glass, stones, shards. This was the second line of the front, in Sheik Maqsoud. One of those times when you don't know what's going on. The bombing had ended a couple of hours ago, the air was still thick with smoke, and a manhunt, street by street, had begun. The rebels were searching for *shabía*. One by one.

But all I remember is the asphalt.

All I know is I suddenly found myself on the ground. I went across last, on the run, the sniper firing from our left, from a hospital. Or something like that.

All I know is that I found myself on the ground.

I realized afterward that he'd hit me.

When I got up again and crawled behind a car.

And my knee. It was all dust and blood.

All scorched.

I don't know why he didn't shoot again.

Stanley says it was a stray bullet. Because it grazed me.

Or maybe the sniper saw the veil, under the helmet. That moment of surprise.

And I was already on the other side.

I don't know.

All I remember is the asphalt.

Just those three seconds—three, five. I don't know. A lifetime.

Nose on the asphalt.

Those three seconds when I thought

I thought

How could you have left me here?

Where the fuck are you? Where the fuck did you all go?

SO THAT'S WHY I'm here now. With my knee bandaged, limping around Antakya a little dazed, somewhat sad, somewhat bewildered. A little empty. I read. I read something entirely different, I read a novel. Partly because there is no one left. And of the few who are left, Lorenzo shows up, looks at my knee, and says: "And there wasn't even anything to write about."

And so I read.

I read and toss down cappuccinos at the Ozsut Café, a café for foreigners here. All shiny. One of those cafés you'll find anywhere in the world, where if you ask for a biscotto, all they have is a muffin, and wherever you are, no matter what country you're in, they'll serve you a fake American breakfast with scrambled eggs. They even have maple syrup—and you thought only Donald Duck used it—and banana cake too, and at nine in the morning they're already listening to Justin Bieber. But a young woman wrote to me. A girl I don't know, a certain Martina, she must be twenty years old or so. She's studying anthropology at the Sapienza. The university in Rome. She wrote to me because she reads me, and, because readers are sometimes weird, she sent me a list of the things she loves to do. To me, though I don't even know her. I don't know why. A list of things she loves to do. And this list has things like driving at night with the car windows open. At night. To me, who at night . . . My first thought was: But they'll shoot you at night, are you crazy?

Windows open.

At night.

I thought: How many years has it been since I've driven at night with the windows open?

And so here I am at the Ozsut. Because I used to love coffee, before all this. Maybe it was the thing I loved most. Chatting with friends in cafés. Especially those on the sea, or

on a lake, a beautiful café on Lake Piediluco, once, a luminosity
I'd never seen before, the kind of radiant light you then keep
looking for all your life, at every café you visit. And though
Antakya doesn't have a lake, it has a river, and the Ozsut has
all these windows overlooking the river, the people strolling.
Strange people who don't explode, don't slump to the ground.
Don't get incinerated.

And so I hang out at the Ozsut.

Which is a curious place. Only foreigners and Syrians.
Because by now everyone knows that only we journalists
come here, and so the others are all Syrians. They sit there
with their banana cake, a slice of apple pie, at the table next to
yours, and you study, write. At some point one of them leans
over your table, from behind, and tells you: "I have a child
soldier." Like that, in your ear. He says: "And he's the son of a
shabìa! Do you want the son of a *shabìa*?" he asks you. "No one
has him." And the journalists, especially the ones who spend
one week in Syria, one week in the Congo, who when the war
in Libya starts again say, "Awesome!" the journalists say: "Do
you have a suicide bomber too? I need a suicide bomber, possibly drunk." That's always the way. With these Syrians who
volunteer as "fixers." A fixer is someone who arranges everything. A logistician. And so they volunteer to be your fixer. To
act as your driver, your interpreter. Your cook. Anything you
want, even though their English is generally limited to "*the cat
is under the table, the rebel is on the chair,*" and it sometimes happens
in Aleppo that they tell you "left" instead of "right"—and on
your left there's a sniper.

Since Abdallah was killed, that's how things have been.

And the other day in Aleppo, I was almost attacked because
of a story going around: Paul Wood's interview with the rebel

who ate his enemy's heart.* Abu Sakkar. A psychopath fea-
tured in a YouTube video where he's feasting on the body of
an enemy, and Paul, who is the BBC correspondent for the
Middle East, and therefore more punctilious than anyone,
and hates these things that are a little like the movies, explains
that it's not clear whether what the rebel has in his hand is
actually a piece of heart, or liver, maybe, or lung. He's inclined
to think it's lung. And of course it's not as if it weren't news-
worthy. Only it became *the* news. All over the world. From
Chile to China, like the story about Guevara. And like the
photo of that child, a month ago, who was smoking a cigarette,
a Kalashnikov slung over his shoulder. A photo that outraged
all of Syria. Because it's one thing to have a weapon slung over
your shoulder, and another thing to shoot it. A child soldier
is not just a child who's at the front, he's a child who's fighting
at the front. Whereas the child in the photo is seven years
old, and at seven years of age you don't have the strength for
a Kalashnikov; it's a contrived photo. But in the meantime it
ended up on the front page. All over the world. While no one
gives a damn about the 101,000 dead. Like this other story,
Abu Sakkar. Because Paul is Paul, he's one of the finest in the
business, and there he was scrutinizing it to see whether it
was the heart or the liver, or maybe the lung, weighing every
word, every adjective, to cushion it as much as possible. And
you could see very well that he was saying: "I'm here because I
have to be." But a cannibal is a cannibal, the BBC is the BBC,
and it suddenly seems that the rebels are all animals. And
you'd like to replace Assad with them? Russia immediately

---

* Paul Wood, "Face-to-face with Abu Sakkar, Syria's 'heart-eating cannibal,'" *BBC
News Magazine*, July 5, 2013.

sneered at the United States, with Saudi Arabia threatening not to finance anyone anymore.

It's growing more and more difficult to work here.

Domenico Quirico from *La Stampa* disappeared on the border with Lebanon.

Yet there is a story in this, it's clear: a man who eats his enemy's heart. But it's also clear that it's a story that will have unpredictable effects, much more powerful than the story deserves—the story of a psychopath, nothing more. An individual who represents no one. Not even the most radical of rebels. A story that could be Syria or someplace in the U.S., say Milwaukee.

And so here I am.

Why—I don't know.

With this knee, besides.

Those three seconds. And to be honest I sometimes wonder what's the point. In the evening, when I'm sitting in front of the TV news, and all I see are dead bodies, corpses and grief, mothers devastated, and maybe it's Syria, maybe Iraq, maybe it's another war, I couldn't say: all I see are dead bodies. And I don't know.

I think about Atmeh. Because there was this girl in Atmeh. On a frayed mat. A girl with Down's. And Atmeh was already what it was, the cold, the hunger, and that girl, in that dilapidated tent, in the mud, humming a singsong cadence. In the silence there in Atmeh, in the snow, only that singsong. Those grunts. She was—she was Syria. That look. Defenseless. Stricken. She was the icon of Syria. It could have been one of those photos that go around the world. With everything after remaining as before. Alessio had looked at her. Focused. Then he looked again: not through the lens.

At the girl. Outside the photo.
And he focused again. He looked again.
The girl wasn't even aware.
In that corner, in that fetid air.
Nothing more. And Alessio there, looking at her. The girl.
The icon.
The girl. And she there, not even aware.
The icon.
He unscrewed the lens. He said—No.
And he walked away.
It was his last time in Syria.

THEY FOUND Eva's son.
The Genovese boy. He had his passport with him.
And then they phoned his father.
His closest friend, they told him, a Somali boy, had been wounded. And Ibrahim tried to drag him to safety. He was shot and killed.
"My son is a hero," the father said.
"My son was a little fool," the mother said.
His name was Giuliano, actually. Giuliano Delnevo. He studied a bit, worked a bit. With no specific plans. He had converted to Islam in 2008, and went around in a beard, robe, and turban. On YouTube there's a video in which he talks about Ramadan, another in which he urges Monti, Italian prime minister at the time, to withdraw troops from Afghanistan. That's all. He urges Monti to build schools and hospitals instead. Much like the campaign against the F-35. Except that now there are all these other more radical videos circulating on his YouTube channel, the Liguristan. I don't know. To be truthful, looking

at him, listening to him, he honestly seems like someone who became an Islamist the way another kid might become a *punkab-bestia*, a gutter punk. It depends on who you run into along the way. But now, of course, the Italian newspapers have discovered Syria. More or less. Because when I went to read the article, the subtitle reported: "Killed in Qusayr, Just Outside of Aleppo." And Qusayr is 125 miles from Aleppo. So I stopped reading. I turned to the following article, about Afghanistan. But I ended up not reading that one either. Maybe the reporter thought he was in Afghanistan, but he was wrong, he was 125 miles farther north. He was in Tajikistan.

And I ordered another piece of banana cake.

The Liguristan.

In reality Westerners such as Giuliano, without Muslim roots, are few here. A Belgian guy. A Canadian. There are so few of them that we all know them. The others are second generation guys. Young men from one of those suburbs you can't even get to by tram or subway. And then sociologists wonder why they aren't able to fit in. What may be wrong with Islam. Many of them, honestly, remind you only of a Fabrizio De André ballad—they left to go to war *"per un ideale, per una truffa, per un amore finito male."* Because of an ideal, because they were misled, because of a love that ended badly.* Like countless other soldiers. They are not fanatics. The first thing you think, when you talk to them, is that they come from difficult lives. That the real war, for them, is the one they left behind. Which, of course, does not justify the decision to go to Syria. Some people react in life by shooting, others by adopting orphans. Personally, I have no

---

* The lyrics are from "La collina."

doubt about who the heroes are. Because my only thought, honestly, when I think about these young men, is that this is not their war. Whatever their reasons. There's this piece by John Cantlie, the first of us to have been kidnapped here. A year ago. He manages to escape at some point. Wounded, but he manages to get free and to run away, swiftly, in these woods like the Highlands, he writes, and those men, behind him, shooting at him. A British man chased by two British jihadists. In a Syria like Scotland.

NOW THE PHONE rings constantly. In more than two years of war, 107,000 dead, it's the first time. No, they don't want to know about Qusayr. Where meanwhile the battle rages. Qusayr is the axis of the revolt; it's like Hama, and most of all, it's strategic, it's at the border with Lebanon. It is from Qusayr that the Hezbollah guerillas who support Assad enter, and if Qusayr falls—if Hezbollah establishes itself in Qusayr—Aleppo will be next. But they don't want to know about Qusayr. They want to know if it's true that there's an Italian woman among the rebels.

An Italian woman at the front. In Aleppo.

Because in fact, there is.

She's thirty years old, and also has a degree. A beautiful woman.

Yes, there's an Italian woman at the front.

And so the phone rings constantly.

They all want to talk to the jihadist woman. Their voices excited. A Jihadist. Italian. "And a woman too!" They're in a state of fibrillation. They want a photo of her with a Kalashnikov. Of her helping her wounded comrades. A photo of her putting on makeup there among the sandbags. With a mirror propped up on the ammunition crates. Of her in high heels, one of them tells me. In the evening, when she goes home. Excuse me, when she goes home where? "Okay," he says, "a photo in flats will also be fine. But does she have a Taliban boyfriend as well?"

For three days. Calls like that.

They all want the Italian woman at the front.

The only problem is that she isn't fighting. They say she fought for only a few days. At first. Some shrapnel to the stomach changed her mind. She, too, thought it was probably wiser to be 22 million against one than stand there in flip-flops against the fighter jets. And so she remains at the front, sure. On the front line. And for nearly two years, true. But she doesn't fight. She deals with humanitarian aid, logistics. Intelligence. "I'm sorry, but she really doesn't fight." "So okay, fudge the answer." "Meaning? A person either fights or doesn't fight." "Meaning you ask her, and she responds with silence. With an ambiguous look. And the reader gets it." "Gets what?" "He understands whatever he wants to understand." "But I've already asked her. And she didn't respond with silence. I asked her: 'Do you still fight?' She said: 'No.' That wasn't an ambiguous look. It was a no."

Lorenzo shows up.

They're offering 2,000 euros for the piece.

Only Lorenzo doesn't have her number.

I tell him: "There's nothing to write about."

"If they pay you, there's a story."

Three days of it.

While Qusayr falls.

While in Qusayr, in the meantime, everything explodes.

Explodes and topples.

And Qusayr isn't just any city here. For anyone. Because it provides access to Homs. And for the Syrians—as well as for us—Homs is where it all started. It was in Homs, on the outskirts of that city, that a mortar struck Marie Colvin and Remi Ochlik. Colvin wrote for the UK's *Sunday Times*, and the only thing someone can say about her is: read what she has written. She was simply number one. Ochlik, twenty-eight years old and a photographer, was considered the best of our generation. One of those faithful to Robert Capa, who used to say that if the photo isn't good, it means you didn't get close enough. That's how Remi was: when everyone else was running away, he was running into it. He was extraordinary.

February 22, 2012.

The bombing was so heavy that the bodies lay there for days. Seven people died retrieving them.

But now, May 2013, the regime is back on the offensive. With intense shelling. Hour after hour, dramatic images filter through, hundreds and hundreds of Syrians trapped while from here all the rebel brigades converge toward the south in a desperate defensive attempt. But Hezbollah is much stronger, and hour after hour, photo after photo, these horrific images multiply. They're all dying in Qusayr, nothing but corpses, corpses, corpses, rubble and blood, and these photographs of nights lit by bombs, these orange-tinged nights, completely ablaze, like the mouth of a steelworks, a blast furnace that will incinerate everything. You call the activists and you hear screams in the background, shots and bombs; you call back after an hour and another voice answers: the first person you talked to is dead.

Hour after hour. Minute after minute.

These excruciating emails. They're killing us all! Where are you? They're killing us all!

But from here Qusayr is too far away. It's too far south.

And for months now the border with Lebanon has been sealed by Hezbollah.

While around you, at the Ozsut, they're listening to Justin Bieber.

I call a general in the Free Army and inquire about the possibility of going in with them. But he has no idea what's going on in Qusayr. He has no idea how he can help me. He says: "We're in Aleppo, Idlib, Raqqa. But farther south, we have no contacts." I call the delegate of the National Coalition with whom I have tighter relations. He's lived in Europe for over twenty years, and has been a guest several times at my place in Tuscany. He goes back and forth from Beirut. He replies from the Amalfi Coast. He tells me not to get so upset. He tells me that when the assault is over, I can go in, of course. A matter of days, he says. Why go in now? Wait for it to be over. Among other things, he says, there's a beautiful exhibit in Rome. He says that maybe he'll pass by my house on the way from Pisa to Florence. I tell him my neighbor has the keys. He says: "I thought you'd be there." Disappointed. He adds: "If you have a girlfriend, I'm with a buddy of mine."

There's nobody left. "Besides, with this light, you can't shoot anything anymore," Tom says, zipping up his backpack. "I need skies with less light."

"Why not go to Brazil?" he tells me. "Or Istanbul. Why don't you go and report on Gezi Park?"

There's nobody left.

I read, in the evening.

I read and look at Alessio's photos. The ones from *Time*.

The ones—the ones I felt like I was falling into the first time I saw them, when I decided to come to Syria. It's been over a year. And this is no longer a revolution. It's—I don't know what it is. And yet there is still a story in them. In those photos. Looking at them all together. There clearly is a story, nothing else has ever been so clear to me.

There is a story.

There is a story, in them.

There are the Syrians.

Even though now there's no one left.

Only those photos.

*We are burnt up by hard facts. Like tradesmen we understand distinctions, and like butchers, necessities.**

---

* Remarque, op.cit., 122.

We're running. We're running quickly between the houses in Salaheddin, now in ruins, these houses that are nothing but rubble and rats, nothing but caked blood, we're running, quickly, from house to house, through the breaches in the foundations, the ones the snipers use, through gaps in the walls, from room to room; we're running, quickly, running through these apartments that are like dig sites, strewn with objects still intact, still in place, except they're all grimy now, covered in dust, and we run and run, from room to room, from floor to floor, staircases that, suddenly, jut out of thin air, because everything has collapsed, all gone, just these stairs there, now, you turn around and there's nothing left anymore, abruptly, only rubble, just more rubble, and so we run, turn back, run quickly, this chopper over our heads, the clatter getting closer, and there are mortars, all around, bullets, nothing but mortars and bullets and we're running from house to house, running quickly, running in the midst of these charred bodies, these intact charred bodies, an entire family at supper, completely black, and everything is normal in the room, everything in its place, the chandelier, the sofa, the china closet, the dinner plates, everything intact, the clock, only it's all grimy with dust, and these six bodies, at the table, composed, fork in hand, still chatting, these six charred bodies, eyes wide, sockets empty, these skeletons, and us running, running, the helicopter slinking low between the streets, hunting for us, hunting for the last ones still alive, while everything, all around us, explodes, explodes and collapses, and there's only this helicopter hunting us, only we are running from room to room, floor to floor, quickly, and we can't stop, because if you stop, before turning, before taking another flight of stairs, if you stop to make sure that there are no snipers on the other side, someone grabs you from the rubble, grabs you by the ankles, pulls you to the ground, these bodies, pleading, "Water, water," they beg, gripping your ankles, pulling you to the ground, but the chopper is over our heads and it's hunting us, it's seen us, it saw us and we have to run, just run, fast, because there's also a plane now, a jet, and it goes into a nosedive, the plane, spins into a nosedive, it saw us, it rushes at us and . . .

Brightness.

Brightness.

3:37.

It's 3:37. Only 3:37 a.m.

A pine tree. A pine tree outside the window. A swing set.

The swing, the hills.

Ramallah.

Ramallah. Back again.

Ramallah.

For months now I haven't slept.
For months now I wake up at the same time.

"I like starting with a word," Federico wrote me, "and following with other, freely associated words." He wrote: "Weightless, Spontaneous, Airy, Vibrant. Soaring."

He wrote to me from Newcastle, where he teaches at the university. Ancient History. And because readers are indeed sometimes strange, he asked me to send him a word for each letter of the alphabet. But in the end I'm here for them, for the readers. Here *with* them, because they play a part in what I write; ultimately, they are the ones who complete it, who construct its significance, its value. They are part of me. And so, even though they're sometimes strange, I thought up a word for each letter of the alphabet.

Freely associated.

Red. R for Red. R for Rebels and for Regime and for Rubble, A for Airplane, H for Helicopter, E for Explosions, M for Mortars, W for Wounded, B for Blade, G for Grief. I for Inadequate. F for Fear, D for Depletion. I for Inadequate and Insufficient. F for Front, F for Freezing, for Famished, for Flight. G for Guilt. C for Corpse, T for Tank, S for Sniper. F for Flesh. C for Collapse.

L for Loneliness.

B for Blood. B for Blood, S for Shrapnel, L for Loneliness.

Loneliness.

I reread the list and came to Ramallah.

Ramallah because this is where I first came. For my Master's thesis, a Master's degree in Human Rights and Conflict Management, and I was supposed to stay three months.

Instead I stayed three years. And when I think of a home anywhere in the world, when I think of the place I most naturally
feel like a foreigner, as Italo Calvino said, I think of Ramallah.* Of Israel and Palestine.

And so I came back.

After more than two years.

Because when I'm in Ramallah I don't feel like I'm dis-
tracting myself with irrelevant things. Like I'm wasting my
time. When I talk to Israelis and Palestinians, I never feel
like I'm gliding over things. I have a feeling of depth. In this
connection, this cohabitation, in this daily confrontation
with life, with basic life, liberty, dignity. Identity. With who I
am. With courage and fear. This being asked to choose, each
day, and each day being given the chance to be like the girl
in that U2 song, "Grace," to turn hurt not into hatred and
acrimony—not into a shield or barricade or assault—but into
openness toward others and understanding. Into gentleness
and beauty. Into kindness. *"She makes beauty out of ugly things..."*
The ability to respond with beauty to what has hurt you—
"what left a mark no longer stings"—means it can no longer hurt
you. "Grace," that's the name of the song. "Grace." And it's the
only thing that I aspire to in life.

That song. Only I got lost.

I don't know where, but I got lost.

I'm beginning to be like all the others. Like those I criticize
so much.

The same catchy phrases meant to be sensational. The

---

* "The ideal place for me is the one in which it is most natural to live as a foreigner." Italo Calvino, *The Uses of Literature: Essays* (New York: Harcourt Brace & Company, 1987), 341.

same superficiality. And when I plan my pieces, when I decide what to report on, I start looking for characters, instead of people.

I begin—I begin to know in advance what I'm going to write. What I'll find.

I begin to see the same things over and over. I begin to use the same words over and over. The same adjectives. I get formulaic. I begin to not feel.

In February, in Aleppo, I was at the entrance to Zarzous, the hospital that replaced al-Shifa. I was there waiting for the victims of a missile, or a sniper—because that's my job. Spending three hours in front of a hospital waiting for someone to die. And all the while I was talking with some kids and another journalist, a dead body lay beside us. I hadn't noticed it.

I noticed it after twenty minutes.

I said: "A body."

And I went on chatting.

The truth is that it doesn't only happen as a journalist. One evening in March, as we were dividing up our apple into nine pieces, the Syrians, as usual, were asking me: "Why doesn't the world intervene?" And I talked about Russia, Obama, Iraq, the politics, but mainly the economic crisis. The recession. There I was telling them: "We can't afford it. We can't help you." Telling them: "The banks. The stock market, mortgages. People in our country can't make it to the end of the month." And they look at you, with their little piece of apple in hand, all of them emaciated, holding cups of yellowish rainwater, they look at you, these people whose problem it is to make it to tomorrow, while your jeans alone cost as much as a whole paycheck. It's not an exaggeration. Your jeans really do cost as much as a paycheck which in Syria supports six people.

And yet you tell them: "We can't afford it. I swear. We really can't."

And so I came back to Ramallah.

Because for months now, there has been only Syria. For months I've written about Syria, read about Syria, lived and breathed Syria. And criticized everyone who didn't cover Syria. 110,000 deaths, 1,976,835 refugees—what else should you write about? What else should you think about?

It seems inhuman to me.

What else can be more important to you, to all of you? What is more urgent than Syria?

But then you get these emails from readers. From South Sudan, from Mexico. From the Central African Republic. From Iraq. Or even just from Taranto, from the Tamburi neighborhood in Taranto where the Ilva steelworks is, where dioxin was even found in breast milk. And it doesn't seem like a war in Taranto, though people are dying of cancer, because their deaths are deferred. And yet there you are, always talking about Syria. With your finger pointed at the indifferent individuals in the world. You who are surrounded by wars which you know nothing about. Somalia. Mali. Drones. The CIE (Center for Identification and Deportation).

The CIE in Bari is located right outside the airport.

Like everyone else, I ignore it.

I write about other things, talk about other things.

Yet there it is: to my left each time I leave for Syria, with its barbed wire, its iron gates. Right there. With its concrete walls.

Invisible.

With its blood on the walls.

While someone, at this moment, is trying to tell me about

it, I'm sure, but, distracted, I don't listen. And I try to talk about Syria to someone who, distracted, doesn't listen . . .

And so I came back to Ramallah.

In search of that beauty that is only found here for me. Where when a factory collapses on the other side of the planet, in the midst of their demonstrations, in the midst of their own many problems, you find someone collecting funds for the workers in Bangladesh.

And if you're sad, someone always notices that you are sad.

Because the world you live in here is always a little more generous.

Ramallah.

Except that I'm in an unfamiliar city. The first photo I took here in 2007 was of a young boy drinking rainwater from a reservoir. Now that reservoir is the swimming pool at the Mövenpick hotel, $200 per night. Now Ramallah has traffic lights. Traffic lights and street lamps. And basalt paving stones downtown. It has trees, flowers, and shrubs. New model cars. And evenings turn into nights to a soundtrack of hit music in these shiny cafés with their cheesecake, apple pie, and banana cake, and if you ask for a Turkish coffee, they say: "Sorry, only Illy." They tell you that in English, even if you asked for it in Arabic. Because you get to Ramallah as you always do. From Jerusalem. You go to Jerusalem and from Jerusalem you take a minibus, which now is no longer a minibus but a coach with air conditioning. The place you leave from is no longer a dusty plaza, but a station, and the checkpoint that separates Ramallah from Jerusalem, the Wall, is now marked by a sign, all shiny, that reads: Qalandia Bus Stop. This is where you get out and they search you, and you cross over to the other side between bomb-sniffing dogs.

Well, so I wake up every night at 3 a.m. I wake up and look at the monument to the resistance in the square below my window. It's a pole. A pole with a Palestinian climbing up, attaching a flag to the top. Because during the Intifada, you ended up in jail if you waved a flag. It was a crime. And so the monument, now, is a pole. And the pole stands in a fountain. I mean an actual fountain with water. Which is always the first thing you notice, at the airport in Tel Aviv: the airport's fountain. Because water, which is scarce here, is one of the most contested issues between Israelis and Palestinians. The Wall's route in Israel encompasses not only the settlements, but also the water reserves. And so the fountain is the first thing you notice. Because the Palestinians, in contrast, don't have water, even today.

Outside of Ramallah.

Because in Ramallah, on the contrary, they have fountains.

In Ramallah they have power.

They don't have a state, but they have a capital.

And a president.

Even though the president doesn't have a passport. He needs Israeli authorization to go and negotiate with the Israelis. But they also have Independence Day.

The only thing that matters today in Ramallah is making money.

This city which was the beacon of the Middle East. Which everyone, when they were under the Mubaraks, under the Gaddafis, suffering submissively, wanted to be like. Like the Palestinians. And now that everyone around Ramallah is fighting for freedom, here they're fighting to pay the TV installments.

They're all in debt, the Palestinians. Because at some point it became clear that the peace process was exactly that: a process. Never ending. Negotiations after negotiations. So Salam Fayyad, who was prime minister, decided: Meanwhile we'll construct our state. Right away. Without waiting for the world's permission. He decided: We'll build our institutions, our economy. And we'll apply for admission to the UN. Otherwise, we'll wait another sixty years. And so getting a mortgage, a loan, has become easy as pie here. And everyone has bought a car, a house. Or opened a café for staffers from the NGOs. And some say Israel is satisfied with this. Because people who have a mortgage to pay don't have time to go and blow themselves up in Jerusalem. People who have a life, they say—who have a house, a job, even an iPhone—never mind that they have no freedom—have no desire to destroy their gains with another Intifada. While others, of course, say the opposite. They say it's not real wealth, because the Palestinian economy depends structurally on that of Israel, and in any case it's only a minority who are wealthy: only four fountains, while the rest don't have water. And so they say just the opposite: that there will soon be another Intifada.

Because Palestine is complicated.

In the meantime, though, here I am. At my favorite café, La Vie, where we are all journalists or aid workers glued to our Macs, all blond, from the West, with Birkenstocks. The only Palestinians are the waiters. Then someone, with his iced frappe, predictably says to the person sitting beside him: "Do you know she's come from Syria?" And the other one replies: "No, really? Awesome!"

I sit here and I read. I read and it never seems to end, because suddenly everything is in turmoil. It began in Turkey with protests over the demolition of a park in Istanbul; not

so much because of the trees, of course, but because the
shopping center that will replace the park is somewhat symbolic of the Islamist party in power, and how it exercises that
power without consulting anyone. Because Turkey is complicated. A Muslim country, yet secular. And above all, an
extremely dynamic country with strong economic growth.
Only it ultimately lacks an opposition party, and freedoms
such as freedom of speech and freedom of the press aren't
very well protected. And so, whether the dispute is over
trees or the constitution, the only way to protest is to take
to the streets. And at the time eleven people were killed.
Then Egypt exploded, with a coup that nobody calls a coup
but which is of course a coup, because Morsi, president of
the Muslim Brotherhood, is a democratically elected president, but now he's in prison, though no one knows where,
no one knows why, without even a lawyer, while the head
of the army occupies his office. So of course it's a coup. No
one would have had any doubts if the Muslim Brotherhood
had overthrown a democratically elected president. And
so Egypt, too, exploded. And Egypt is terribly complicated
right now, with all these revolutionaries who one year ago
chose Morsi at the elections so they wouldn't have a president from the old regime, and now, to get rid of Morsi, they
are choosing the old regime. At the moment, all we know
is that the number of deaths in Cairo is in the hundreds.
And even in Tunisia now, where secularists and Islamists are
in power together and it seemed like an ordinary transition
was underway—some disturbances but nothing special—
even there the leader of the opposition was shot the other
day. So here we all are glued to Al Jazeera, watching Cairo
burn. All of us at a loss because Libya is in a state of anarchy

with all its militias, Syria is what it is, and now even Egypt and Tunisia have fallen into chaos.

And without Egypt and Tunisia—what's left?

Because it's not as if the rest of the Middle East is any better off. Because, to be clear, the main supporter of the rebels in Syria—the main supporter of democracy—is Saudi Arabia. Which doesn't even have a real parliament, and which I'll never be able to write about because to go there I need a male guardian. So either find me a husband who will take me there on a leash, or I will never be able to tell you about this country, champion of freedom in Syria.

Well, so, things are a bit of a mess these days. Everywhere you turn. And where things seem to be going well, it's only because they haven't begun to flare up.

And so here we all are, glued to Al Jazeera, watching Cairo burn.

And no one knows where to start.

This morning, one after the other, within a few miles' range: Ramallah is in turmoil because three boys were killed in Qalandia. A rocket was launched from Lebanon, as part of the constant war against Israel, while as part of another war—since Lebanon is now also experiencing a war between pro-Assad and anti-Assad factions—a car bomb exploded in Beirut. And as a result Israeli planes are over Lebanon this morning, helicopters are over the West Bank, and drones are over Gaza, because, as usual, the Gaza border has been closed and people are locked inside, starving, and rockets are raining down from there too. And the Israelis also bombed Syria yesterday, a weapons depository. And in Cairo, they're shooting in the streets. And it's only 11:27 a.m.

It was December 17, 2010, when Mohamed Bouazizi, twenty-six, a street vendor selling fruits and vegetables, was stopped by police in southern Tunisia. He had no license, and when they confiscated his pushcart, he set himself on fire. Because that was all he had. Only that cart. That's how it all started. With a generation that decided it had nothing left to lose. "But now the military and the Islamists are vying for power, a power won with our blood, while we are on the fringes. Again. Too divided to reclaim a place. And too depleted. Because we have no work, no nothing. The priority for many is simply to find something to eat," Wael Abbas, one of the leaders of Tahrir Square, tells me from Cairo.

D for Disheartened and Divided. S for Scattered.

"And no matter where you turn in the Middle East, it is no different. Crisis everywhere."

C for Confused and Crushed.

D for Defeated.

"You are lucky to be from Italy," he tells me.

He says: "Here a person studies, he earns a degree, and he knows it is useless. That he will never find work."

Or have rights.

That he will never count for anything.

Because power is all corruption and collusion, he says. "And they keep telling you they lack the funds—the funds for hospitals, for schools—but they always find the funds for weapons. And they call it poverty, they call it a crisis, when instead it's about inequality."

He says: "You are lucky to come from Italy."

He tells me that.

And I read. I'm reading La Repubblica.

Marco Cacciatore was also twenty-six years old. All he wrote was: "I am ashamed. I can't even buy cigarettes." And he shot himself.

He was unemployed. And so were his parents.

And he shot himself.

In Milan.

Where things appear calm only because they have never got started. Among those of us who have nothing left to lose, all without work, without dignity—all perpetual temporaries, by day a biologist, in the evening a waiter, Saturday a gardener. All disheartened and divided—we who criticize the Arab Spring, asking, What did they gain? Wars and dictatorships. We who are so good at not failing only because we are so good at not trying.

THEN HE FINALLY wrote to me. My boss, that is. After more than a year, a bout of typhus and a bullet to the knee, he saw a clip on television and thought the kidnapped Italian woman was me. And he finally wrote: "If you have Internet, couldn't you tweet about the capture?"

I mean, a person gets home in the evening—though "gets home" aren't exactly the right words in Syria, with these mortars exploding all around you, the dust, the hunger, the fear. A person takes a break in the evening at a rebel base in the midst of the inferno, and hopes to find a friend on email, a word, a hug, and instead finds only Elena, who is on vacation in her house and has written eight messages marked "Urgent!" because she can't find the spa pass. I mean, eight times, and the rest are notes from readers scattered around, messages like this one from Paolo: "Beautiful piece, reminds me of your book on Iraq." Only my book isn't about Iraq. It's about Kosovo.

I don't know. The only thing I know for sure is that people

have this romantic image, right? The freelance journalist ready to give up the security of a steady paycheck in exchange for the freedom to follow the stories she most wants to follow. But you're not free by any means. Quite the opposite. You're driven by front-page news. The truth is that the only chance I have of working, today, is to stay in Syria. That is, to stay where no one else wants to stay. After Italian, the second second-language in Aleppo, and in particular at the front, is Spanish, because at this point the Greeks don't have enough money to pay for plane tickets. And then all the editors ask you for is blood, all they want is bombing. I mean, you report on the Islamists and their entire network of social activities, you describe the reasons for their strength, a much more difficult piece than writing about the front, and you try to explain, not just sensationalize, and they tell you: "But here in six thousand characters nobody died."

Actually I should have realized it when they asked me to do a piece from Gaza, because Gaza, as usual, was being bombed and because, the email said, you know Gaza by heart. What sense does it make for you to stay in Aleppo? But I came to Syria, I said, because I saw the photos taken by that guy, Alessio Romenzi, in *Time*, the photographer who crept into the water pipes and crawled out in Homs when nobody even knew Homs existed. And one day I saw those photos, while I was listening to Radiohead: I saw those looks, so direct, I swear, eyes that bored into me, because they were under siege in Homs and Assad was exterminating them, one by one, and no one even knew Homs existed, and—and I swear to God, those photos stung my conscience and in the end all I could say was: I have to go to Syria. Right away. I *must* go to Syria. And it turns out the most frustrating thing is that writing from Aleppo is no different than writing from Rome. You're paid the same: $70 for each piece. In places where everything costs three times as much, because in war people speculate, and to sleep in Aleppo, say, under mortar fire, on a mattress on the floor and with yellow water that tomorrow will give me another round of typhus, costs $50 per night. A car is $250 a day. The result is that you end up maximizing rather than minimizing the danger. Because not only can you not afford insurance, almost a thousand dollars a month, but in general you can't afford a "fixer," that is, a local who will see to your logistics, the arrangements, and you can't afford an interpreter either. You find yourself in a foreign city completely on your own. In the midst of flying bullets. And in the newsrooms they are perfectly aware that with $70 per piece you are forced to cut back on everything, hoping you'll die if you're hit, because you could never afford to be wounded. Still, they buy your piece. Even though they would never buy a Nike soccer ball sewn by a Pakistani child. Like the time in Castelvolturno, when the migrant workers went on strike. I got this email: "I want a piece that's outraged! 50 euros! They only make 50 euros per day! What kind of a world is it?" While there we all were getting paid 20 euros each for that piece.

And then with these new technologies, there's this idea, right? This basic misunderstanding that information equals speed: a race to see who's first to plant a flag on the moon. And so it goes without saying that the agencies, the Reuters, are unbeatable. Yet it's a self-defeating logic. Because that way you end up with redundant material, and your newspaper has no angle: there's no reason why I should pay to read you. I mean, I have the Internet for news. Free. I demand more of a newspaper. I demand analysis, I demand in-depth coverage—I demand the ability to understand, not only to be informed. Because the crisis today has to do with the newspapers, not the readers. The readers are out there, and contrary to what the editors think, they are intelligent readers who want intelligent pieces. Simplicity, which is not to say simplification. Because every time I publish a sensational piece, I always find a dozen emails afterward, people telling me, "Yes, but," "great piece," "a superb depiction, but I want to understand what's happening in Syria." And I would love to explain that I can't write an analysis, because if I try to analyze the situation, they will reject my piece, saying, "Who do you think you are?" Even though I have two undergraduate degrees, a Master's, two books, and ten years of war experience behind me, and my youth truly ended with the first war I covered. But the truth is that as freelancers we are second-class journalists. Even though we are all you find in Syria, because Syria is a bastard war, a war of the last century, a trench war fought with gunfire, never mind drones. It's a war fought inch by inch, street by street, and it's terrifying, shit, it's terrifying because there you are writing with your iPad, writing while everything around you is exploding and—and still they treat you like a kid. You take a photo worthy of the front page or a cover and they tell you: "You just happened to be in the right place at the right time." You write an exclusive piece, like the one about the mosque, which Stanley and I were the first to enter, and they say: "How can I justify the fact that my correspondent wasn't able to get in and you were?" One editor wrote to me: "I'll buy it but he'll get the byline."

And you're a woman. So they're always asking you to write about women. Sure, that time when I wasn't wearing the veil under my helmet and they were all men inside taking shelter, and they left me out under the mortars. Sure. It's my most cited piece. But truthfully it was only that one time. It's the other journalists, all men, I swear, who are always telling me: you're not covered up enough, you're not sitting modestly enough, your eyes aren't meek enough, you don't respect the local culture enough, and on and on—even though they've never opened a Koran. Like Jonathan that evening: they were bombing everything, and there I was huddled in the corner with that look that—what other look can you have?—that look that says maybe you'll be dead in a minute, and Jonathan comes in, glances at me, and says: "This is no place for a woman." What can you say to someone like that? You idiot, this is no place for anyone? It's a sign of mental sanity if I'm terrified, because Aleppo is falling. The guys are all traumatized: Henri talks about nothing but war, Ryan is zonked out on amphetamines, and yet each time a child is torn apart, you're the only one they come to, asking, "How are you holding up?" Because you're a woman and fragile. And you feel like answering, "I'm holding up as well as you are." Because the times I look distressed, in fact, are the times that I defend myself by pulling out every emotion, every feeling. They are the times I save myself.

People think: Syria? But it's a madhouse. A guy who can't find a job enlists in Al Qaeda and there's his mother chasing him through Aleppo to beat him up. A Japanese tourist at the front who is actually on vacation, I swear. There really is a Japanese tourist in Aleppo, and he really is at the front. His name is Toshifumi Fujimoto, honest to God, and he says he needs two weeks of adrenaline a year. Then there's the Swede, a recent law graduate, who with his pen and Moleskine has come to gather evidence of war crimes, and he wanted to get to Damascus by hitchhiking. Or the American musicians with bin Laden beards—"So we'll look like Syrians," they say—even though they're blond and six feet tall. They've brought medicine for malaria, though malaria hardly exists in Aleppo, and they want to distribute it while playing music, kind of like the Pied Piper. Not to mention various UN officials scattered here and there. You tell them there's a child with leishmaniasis, "Can we treat him in Turkey?" No we can't, the email apologizes, since it's a specific child and we can only deal with children in general.

And then there's us. Because you're a war reporter, and in the end you're always a head above the others, right? With that hero's aura, that invincible quality, you who risk your life to give the voiceless a voice. The last of the white knights, you who have seen things that others have never seen. You are a gold mine of stories; at dinner you're the awesome guest, and people vie to have you over, and—and then you get there and discover equivocation everywhere. And everywhere you go, this mantra crops up: *It's confidential.* Because instead of networking, putting up a united front, creating a union, here where everything is already so difficult, we are our own worst enemies. And that's the reason the $70 per piece is not the result of lack of funds. Because there are always funds for a piece about Berlusconi's girlfriends. The real reason is that you ask for $100 and someone else is ready to sell for $70. So there's the fiercest competition among us, zero collaboration, zero support. Take Beatriz, for instance, who in April wanted to be the only one to report on a particular rally, so she directed me the wrong way and sent me into the snipers. Into the snipers! Over a fucking rally like a thousand others. And then we say we are here like Romenzi, like Alessio, here so that someday no one will be able to say, "I didn't know." When the only reason we're here is to win an award, to finally get a couple of lines in return from the editor. To gain a foothold among all these photographers who are only chasing after a single shot, the icon, and don't give a damn about the continuity and comprehensiveness of the narrative, about the complete picture. I say photographers solely because the writers are all comfortably situated in Turkey, most of them sprawled out on a couch reporting what the photographers tell them. And we're here on our own, obstructing one another as if we had a Pulitzer-worthy story on our hands. Whereas we have absolutely nothing, caught between a regime that will only issue you a visa if you're against the rebels and the rebels themselves who, like the regime, only allow you to see what they want you to see. It's not as if you're free when you're with them. And the truth is that we're a failure: after two years, readers can barely remember where Damascus is, and the world automatically thinks of Syria as "that Syrian mess," because the world doesn't know anything about Syria, aside from blood, blood, blood. And truthfully that's why the Syrians hate us. Take that recent photo of the child with the cigarette and a Kalashnikov, for instance. It's obvious that the photo is contrived, it's plain as day, and yet it's in all the newspapers now and everyone screams: "Those Syrians! Those Arabs! Those barbarians!" At first people used to stop me in Aleppo to say thank you, thank you for showing the world Assad's crimes; the last time someone stopped me, he said, "Shame on you."

But then I'd be the first. Because if I had ever understood anything about this war, I would not have been afraid to love, afraid to take a chance in life, if only I had really understood anything about Syria, about this life that might end this second, instead of huddling against the wall a thousand times in my dark dank corner while everything around me exploded, instead of cowering there hopelessly regretting everything I had never had the courage to say, now that it was too late, too late for everything, and how could I have lost what was most beautiful to me? Because this is the only thing left to say about a war, the only piece that I really should have written. Now that it's too late, rather than getting sidetracked with rebels, loyalists, Sunni, and Shia, the only thing to understand—the story that remained caught between my fingers: You who are able to, you who are alive tomorrow, what are you waiting for? Why don't you love enough? The only thing to write, from amid my rubble, if only I had understood anything: You who have everything, why are you so afraid?

IN THE END, even if you stay here for months, you'll have only a scattered idea of Syria.

For one thing because you are forced to choose. Choose whether to cover the Syria of Assad or the Syria of the rebels. And obtaining a visa from Assad is essentially impossible. That is, it's possible if you're satisfied with idling around the cafés in Damascus and writing under anesthesia. Writing about the tennis club, about the banker who assures you that everything is normal in Damascus, maybe just a little sadder than usual in the evening, in the restaurants, you know? They don't have the fresh fish they once had. And the 110,000 deaths? It's forbidden to enter Qusayr, Homs. Or Latakia, the city of the Assads, to meet some of those Alawites. Or the outskirts of Damascus, where there is fighting like there is in Aleppo, with everything exploding and toppling. Entry prohibited. But it's not all that much different with the rebels. Not just because they only control scattered bits and pieces of territory, and therefore the war in Daraa, say, to the south on the border with Jordan, is a different war—with different brigades, it's a different world. But because they, too, have their red zones declared off-limits. For instance, Atmeh. The border. The one the Islamists pass through. And you have to pass through it too, to get to Aleppo. But you can't stop. Prohibited.

And so the truth is that even if you stay here for months, you have only a fragmented idea of Syria.

Aleppo, in the end, is only Aleppo.

As for the rest of Syria, you read about it in the papers as you might if you were in Guatemala. In the Andes.

Because the truth is that Syria is inaccessible, even when you're in Syria.

Raqqa, for example. Raqqa is one hundred miles from Aleppo, to the east. Toward Iraq. It has a population of 220,000. And more than 600,000 displaced persons. Because it was considered a marginal city, outside of the war's Aleppo-Daraa corridor, and therefore a safe city; and many people thought of fleeing there. In the middle of the desert. But above all, Raqqa was the first provincial capital out of fourteen to be captured by the rebels. The first and the last. It was captured this year, in February 2013. In twenty days. Not thanks to the Free Army so much, actually, as to a decision by local leaders, who have always been relatively independent from Damascus, and at a certain point sided with the rebels. For one thing, because of its marginal status, Raqqa was guarded by army units that were not particularly spirited, so there was no prolonged battle as in

Aleppo. Three weeks and it was over. But then, since there were no journalists around, the rebels will tell you: we captured Raqqa. But they don't tell you how. Here, if one of the two sides doesn't surrender, the fighting goes on forever, because neither of the two is strong enough to win, but both are strong enough not to lose.

Strong enough to prevent the other from gaining power.

One controls a city while the other goes on dropping bombs.

In any case, Raqqa is now the first city to be entirely controlled by the rebels (while the regime, in fact, continues to bomb). And therefore everyone looks to Raqqa to form some idea of what a Syria without Assad might be like. A free Syria.

Except that power, in Raqqa, was never handed over to the National Coalition. It was never returned to the Syrians. At first it was jointly exercised by the Free Army and by something termed the Religious Council in Support of the Revolution. The outcome: reconstruction was never begun, and not a single dollar went for water or electricity. For bread. For humanitarian aid. Just more and more sharia law. Because the priority, in Raqqa, with six hundred thousand displaced refugees, seems to be to enact laws against high heels and alcohol. To prohibit music and cigarettes. Sharia and looting, extortion, kidnappings: that's what Raqqa is today. Apart from the bombings by the regime.

Because power quickly fell into the hands of the Islamists. At the beginning, as was the case elsewhere, the Islamists had the trust and esteem of many. Unlike the Free Army, they actually tried to govern. To distribute food and medicine, to restore water, electricity. A minimum of public order. But it didn't last long. And not just because of sharia.

Not because of cigarettes. One of the principal brigades, the Ahrar al-Sham, robbed the bank of Raqqa and spent every-thing they stole on weapons. But most of all because Raqqa, along with Deir ez-Zor, farther south, is an oil region. And it's rumored that there is a hush-hush agreement between the regime and the Islamists for the extraction and man-agement of oil. Because everyone needs oil revenues to buy weapons. And while the rebels control the areas with the wells, the regime controls the areas with the pipelines. And so, for once, the regime and the rebels reached an immediate accord. Sunnis and Shiites.

And there are other strange things going on.

For example, Iran's stamp on the passport of one of the rebel commanders.

Iran. Assad's most loyal ally.

And the rebel headquarters, they have never been bombed. *Never.*

And everyone knows where they are. Including me.

Well, strange things. Things that don't add up.

And that's why we journalists are allowed to go to Aleppo, but not to Raqqa.

Not to Deir ez-Zor.

In any case, Al Qaeda controls Raqqa directly now.

The headquarters of the local brigade of the Free Army, the Ahfad al-Rasoul, the Descendants of the Prophet, was hit by four car bombs—for the first time, the Islamists attacked other rebels. And they are attacking more than that: they have set up their headquarters in a church and have hoisted their defiant black flag from the bell tower.

As usual in the Middle East, in Syria minorities are a sketchy subject. The census surveys have never recorded ethnicity and religion: the available figures, 10 percent Christian, more or less, 12 percent Alawite, are merely estimates and approximations. It was the French, in the twenties, during the years of the Mandate, who focused on minorities, in accordance with the typical European policy of *divide et impera*, divide and conquer. In search of allies, they guaranteed the loyalty of the Alawites by promoting them to the highest ranks of the armed forces. With the Assads, then, starting in the seventies, political and economic power was linked to military power. And so today, out of about 200,000 career soldiers, the Alawites number about 140,000 and make up 80 percent of the officers. The two main elite corps in particular, the Republican Guard and the Fourth Armored Division led by Maher, Bashar's brother, are exclusively Alawite.

And so people say: the Alawite regime.

They say: the revolt of the Sunni majority.

Except that Loubna Mrie, in Aleppo, is also Alawite.

Just as Jimmy Shininian, Raqqa's most noted activist, is Christian.

He is twenty-five years old, an engineer. And he is one of the many that we haven't written about while focused on the blood at the front, focused on the easiest things. Except that his freedom also depends on us. Because if you only talk about those who are fighting, any revolution becomes a war.

"I understand," he says. "I realize that for all of you Syria is just one war among many. But for us," he says, "this is our only life—it is not one life among many."

"In Syria, we never had these issues," he says. "Declaring yourself a Christian meant being respected. The denominational conflict was imported by foreign fighters." Who not only fill the ranks of the rebels. Just as the rebels would have been crushed without the jihadists, Assad would not have held out for long without Hezbollah either. "By now, we're merely hostages of somebody else's war. We haven't only lost the revolution. We've lost Syria.

"And it's not true that the Islamists were critical. All the territories they now control were captured by the Free Army. What was taken from Assad here was taken from Assad by the Free Army." And then taken again.

"The vast majority in Raqqa is opposed to an Islamic state, and over half is more than opposed: it is outraged. But there is nothing we can do," he explains. "They're the ones who have weapons."

We heard the same words in Damascus two years ago.

Only then it was in reference to Assad.

THE FIRST PHOTO arrived around five in the morning. A row of bodies.

A father on his knees.

But I've been getting rows of bodies for months now from Syria.

For months I've been waking up at the same time, always to the same bodies. The same fathers on their knees. So I look at them distractedly.

Just another row of bodies.

And then they started resembling the bodies in the river, the ones in February. Because they were all in a row like that: all in order. One after the other. All the same. I buried my head in the pillow again and tried to sleep.

The bodies seemed to be asleep too. One after the other.

All orderly, tidy, all—

All without blood. All without the slightest trace of blood.

Or wounds.

No bullets, bombs. All—

Intact. All intact. And I opened my eyes.

Photos and videos kept pouring in one after another, scores of children lying on the ground, naked, dozens and dozens, gasping, foaming at the mouth, their eyes bulging, runny. They coughed; they coughed and died. They died, and I've never seen anything like it.

Eyes rolled upward, shaken by convulsions, they couldn't be held still. The screaming.

Foaming at the mouth, those bulging eyes. They coughed and died.

I've never seen anything like it.

Because it's August 21, 2013. And that, sweet Jesus, is gas.

ROCKETS WITH CHEMICAL warheads, from what we've understood. Hurled down on Ghouta, on the eastern outskirts of Damascus, during the night. Around two in the morning. A few miles from the bankers at the tennis club. Where they say there are restaurants, cafés, and there's life as usual. Instead for months it's been a quagmire of fighting between rebels and regime, the usual battle in which no one advances.

More than 1,300 dead.

Actually, just a few miles from Ghouta, in Damascus, there are UN inspectors in addition to the bankers these days. At Assad's request. Because it's not the first time: gas has already been used in Syria. Apparently by both sides. The regime is said to have used the gas in Jobar, also near Damascus, in April. Two journalists from Le Monde, who by chance were there under-cover, delivered a sample to a laboratory for blood and tissue testing. The result: sarin. The rebels, however, supposedly used chlorine, a more rudimentary saline solution, in March, in Khan al-Assal, near Aleppo. Which is why Assad turned to the UN. But until now gas has always been used on a smaller scale, resulting in a few dozen deaths, and it is never used alone: always in support of conventional weapons. Always camouflaged by conventional weapons. To arouse no reactions.

Because Obama had stated that this was Syria's red line: chemical weapons.

A year ago he said that the use of chemical weapons "would change my equation."

Meaning his assessment of the need for intervention.

Now the rebels have the strongest incentive to use chemical weapons, the regime's supporters immediately responded. Now the regime has the strongest incentive to use anything but chemical weapons, said the rebels' supporters.

A critically fatal statement spoken lightly, said everyone else.

In any case we will never know the truth. Who it was, this morning. While the UN negotiates to have its inspectors go another ten miles farther into Ghouta, Assad is already bombing everything. And destroying all the evidence.

It's not that the Arabs are more barbaric than anyone else. The biggest gas stockpiles in the world today, though in the process of being dismantled, are still in the United States and Russia. Both of whom signed the Convention for the Prohibition of Chemical Weapons, in 1993,* not because they are

---

* The full name of the treaty, which entered into force in 1997, is the Convention on the Prohibition of the Development, Production, Stockpiling and Use of Chemical Weapons and on their Destruction. It is administered by the Organisation for the Prohibition of Chemical Weapons (OPCW), an intergovernmental organization based in The Hague.

more enlightened than other countries, not in their wars in Pakistan or Chechnya, but as my international law professor Cassese once said, because they don't need it. The reason why Syria has all these deposits of sarin is that gas is the nuclear weapon of the poor. Only Israel, here, has atomic power. So all that's left for the others around them is gas. Or suicide bombings.

You can't understand much about Syria if you don't understand Israel. One reason for the difference between Libya and Syria, between intervention in Libya and nonintervention in Syria, is that Libya doesn't border Israel, while Syria does. And Israel has reached some sort of equilibrium with Assad. Its only problematic border today is with Lebanon. The Assads have always confined themselves to words, whereas to Israel the new Syrian rebels seem a little too Muslim, a little too Arab, and Israel still hasn't decided whether it prefers Assad or the opposition. A safe dictatorship or an unknown democracy.

And the fact that Israel hasn't decided, with this Arab Spring that burst out, unexpected, and above all, indecipherable, is another reason why the United States, with Europe following suit, hasn't acted. They haven't decided either.

That is, they hadn't decided.

Because now, suddenly, everyone has decided.

Now, suddenly, Syria is on the front page.

And journalists are already on their way to Turkey.

"What, you're still at home?" Lorenzo asks me at 3:19 p.m. "Don't tell me you're going to miss the rockets."

Because we all know what's needed now.

We all care about Syria, apparently.

About human rights.

We must bomb.

And yet we had started writing about Syria in February 2012 because we believed the red line had been crossed then. When the peaceful demonstrations against Assad had been leveled by bullets and mortars. But clashes between the regime and the newborn Free Army, little more than boys with Kalashnikovs and flip-flops, quickly flared, and we found ourselves facing another red line, that of war. Fierce fighting, street by street, inch by inch. Just as quickly, the dead began to mount up by the hundreds, by the thousands. And we began telling editors to call us before wrapping up so we could update the figures. Then, all of a sudden, the first foreign fighters arrived. And it seemed like another red line: that of a Syria held hostage to other people's battles and strategies. Until missiles began to rain down on us. Until we saw the command of the Free Army in Aleppo replaced by that of Jabhat al-Nusra, Islamists linked to Al Qaeda. Until we ran into Syrians who were more and more emaciated, sallow, haggard from hunger and typhus, while no one even recorded the death count anymore, since so many weren't even pulled out of the rubble.

We'd crossed the last red line a month ago. In Aleppo. Two children shot for uttering a word against Islam. Because the truth is that the only red line is the trail of blood and gore left by the wounded, their torn bodies dragged away in the dust when—after the missiles, after the mortars—the snipers get their turn, firing on the rescuers.

Interpretations and opinions about the chemical attack, at present, are divergent as usual. What sense did it make for the regime to do it? Assad's defenders ask. After the capture of Qusayr, and now with the explicit support of Hezbollah, Assad is clearly on the upswing. Why give the U.S. an excuse to intervene, especially with UN inspectors right there in Damascus? Not only there in Damascus, but there to investigate another chemical attack, one near Aleppo, for which the major suspects, instead, are the rebels. Who supposedly did it to divert international attention. But in the area of the attack, the regime was in trouble, Assad's opponents argue. It was in danger of having the rebels enter Damascus. And most importantly, his opponents are convinced that while Assad may have an iron grip on the situation, everyone knows that the regime has long been in the process of crumbling. With Bashar flanked and surrounded by multiple centers of power. And the chemical attack might therefore have been carried out without agreement among the leaders, or ordered by leaders competing with Bashar—starting with his brother Maher.

Everyone, these days, spouts an opinion and interpretation.

Revealing who the perpetrator was based on YouTube videos.

But then, truthfully, is it critical to know who it was? Does anyone still doubt that the regime carries out crimes against humanity, or that the rebels commit war crimes? Because there's another red line that we crossed months ago, when the Syrians began fleeing not only from the areas controlled by the regime, but also from the so-called liberated areas, terrorized by anarchy, looting, summary executions, kidnappings, and ad hoc Islamic courts.

What does it matter, chemical weapons or conventional arms? With more than one hundred thousand dead, it's time to act in Syria. Did the father of my friend Fahdi, an Alawite, who died in Latakia for lack of medicine, die because of cancer or because of the war? As Cassese used to say, quoting Mark

Twain, there is always a simple solution to complex problems: the wrong one.

Many people, these days, recall Kosovo. But the only similarity with those seventy-eight days of bombing, it was 1999, is Russia's veto, which now, as then, obstructs the UN and its Security Council. Besides that, the context is radically different. The confrontation between the Albanian majority and Serbian minority does not compare to the tangle of diversity and the plurality of actors and interests that make up Syria. The underlying issue here is that the opposition is heterogeneous and divided, with Islamists as the dominant group. What could be the objective of the bombing, when the real reason for the lack of action on the part of the international community is not the Russian veto but the absence of an alternative to Assad? The war in Kosovo ended with a protectorate that lasted for years. As general Wesley Clark, supreme commander of NATO at the time, recalled, it was the opposite of a shock and awe operation, of two days of bombing like the ones we're talking about now. In any war, he told us, we must have clear political goals, and above all, be prepared for escalation: exactly like what happened in Kosovo, two days that became seventy-eight, until Milosevic surrendered. Except the context of this possible escalation, now, is not Yugoslavia, it's a Middle East where everywhere you look there's a coup, a drone, a car bomb. Ramallah is one of the most inured cities at the present time, and yet, when three Palestinians were killed the other day, the entire West Bank flared up.

Many interpret intervention as a defense of the West's credibility: the use of chemical weapons, it is argued, cannot go unpunished. The word of a U.S. president cannot be ignored. In fact, it all seems very much in keeping with our role in Syria up until now. Because it's not at all true, of course, that we've been absent. Until now, the strategy had been to arm and support the rebels, but not too much, not completely: only up to the point of ousting Assad through a transition that would involve both renewal and stability—with the emphasis on stability. A stability that despite the rhetoric would guarantee Israel a more secure border. Only it didn't work because the opposition proved to be a disaster, because Al Qaeda appeared, because Assad chose to demolish Syria rather than capitulate. Nothing new, then. Contrary to appearances, the impending bombings are yet another "Yes but no" that doesn't answer the fundamental question: What is the alternative to Assad? A man who has caused a million children to become refugees, and who orders airstrikes against the rest.

As for credibility, chemical weapons, prohibited by conventional international law, have been excluded from the jurisdiction of the International Criminal Court. Because they constitute a unique category—weapons of mass destruction—along with biological and, in particular, nuclear weapons, whose possessors are known to all. And so, here we are being outraged over a red line that we have not classified as a war crime, just to reserve the right to cross it. Maybe it should be remembered that while it's true that international crimes exist—that is, crimes that involve individual criminal responsibility—in this case, complicity in international crimes also exists. For example, the sale of arms to those who then use them to commit international crimes. None of these crimes are subject to regulation. You have to be careful to defend your credibility. One day you could be taken seriously.

WELL THEN.

To recap.

In the morning, I now find thirty new editorials for each corpse, a photo from Aleppo, and thirty articles on Syria, and it seems that no place exists in the world except Syria.

Now everyone cares.

And here I am reading admiringly. Because they write all these editorials from New York, Paris, Rome, Honolulu—elegant editorials, not an adjective out of keeping. All these precise, detailed analyses. With no hesitation. And without ever having been in Syria. People think it's easy. But the truth is that writing in Aleppo, from the front, we are all great writers. Even you, if you were to come to the front tomorrow, could come up with a front-page feature, a piece filled with big scenes, adrenaline, rhythm, blood. I'm not kidding. The front is the easiest thing to write about. You just have to make sure you come back alive. What's really hard is writing about Syria if your entire Middle East is the copper plate you bought on vacation in Morocco. Then, sure, you have to be great.

And so here I am reading admiringly. These polished editorials, the Arab Spring, democracy, Jefferson, Rousseau—these editorials that range from the French Revolution to October 1917 in Russia, to the Greeks of course, to Sparta, Athens, Gorbachev, and the Berlin Wall. There's a magnificent parallel drawn this morning, extremely learned, between Egypt and Syria, comparing these Sunnis and Shiites to the Guelphs and Ghibellines, the Girondists and Jacobins. When there are no Shiites in Egypt.

Not one.

We followed the UN inspectors' arrival in Ghouta live, moment by moment, all of us with bated breath, because now

we all care about Syria, and because Assad finally said yes, that
the inspectors could continue on, now that they'd already
come that far, but only to determine whether gas had actually been used, not to determine who had used it. Just to con-
firm that strange things had indeed been happening in Syria
lately, like clouds of gas all of a sudden. In short, while we
were all on Twitter, Britain's Prime Minister Cameron consulted Parliament and Parliament voted no. No to military
intervention. And then Obama decided to consult Congress.
But he must have consulted the polls first, which must not
have been encouraging. Because of the budget bill, actually,
not because of Syria, since the budget had to be approved
within a few days in the U.S. or government spending would
be halted. And so the Republicans, taking advantage of the
tight deadline, upped the ante, and in exchange for a yes on
Syria demanded amendments to health care. Somewhat like
what happened in Italy, right? When at crucial moments, at a
vote critical to the fate of the country, in exchange for a yes,
every deputy wants funding for a parade, for a debate team,
for a Protected Designation of Origin for a local cucumber. In
short, while Obama was busy consulting everyone who could
be consulted, Russia consulted Assad. And asked him to dis-
mantle his chemical arsenal.

That's where we are, more or less. At Russia's initiative. If
Assad gets rid of his chemical arsenal, there will be no bombings. That is, *no bombing of Assad*. Those *by Assad* may continue.
So the U.S. must now consult with Saudi Arabia and the European Union, then the European Union must consult with its
individual members and Saudi Arabia with the members of
the Gulf Cooperation Council. Then all of them—Arabs,
Europeans, and Americans—all of them together will consult

with Russia, after Russia has consulted with Iran. And after they have all then gone ahead and consulted with Turkey—which is neither here nor there on the map and so each time they run the risk of forgetting it completely—then the whole world can finally consult with the UN.

The whole world except the Syrians.

After all, it was only tear gas in the beginning. Tear gas and clubs. Then, one day, bullets. And after the bullets, one day, mortars. From mortars to helicopters. From helicopters to tanks. "In reality, that red line is a green light. It appeases Assad, who except for gas can use any other weapon and no one will react," Abdallah told me on my first morning in Aleppo, when we were up to cannon fire, but the missiles and planes had not yet arrived.

If only we listened to the Syrians sometimes. Abdallah had set up the Media Center to help us foreign journalists, who had in the meantime been writing about a Sunni majority oppressed by the Shiite minority. Although beside him, explaining Syria to us, there was also Loubna, an Alawite.

"It is surprising, honestly, that they are talking about deterrence. Because if the goal is to discourage a return to the use of gas, an American attack is the best incentive to incite those interested in outside intervention to use it. And there are many of them among those who oppose the regime, but also among those within the regime who aim to replace Assad," Mohammed Noor, another veteran of the Media Center, says today. He deals with refugees now, along with many other activists who went from demonstrations to working in the mess halls for internally displaced persons. Because in February Abdallah was killed by the rebels, who don't want journalists around anymore to witness the fact that they are building a new regime, while we continued writing in hope of a revolution for freedom.

Syria is more and more complicated.

But when have we ever listened to the Syrians? Certainly not these days, when all of a sudden the world has started focusing on Syria. And of the dozens of editorials I read, the only thing that comes to mind is an old line attributed to Mark Twain: "God created war so that Americans would learn geography."

Because the entire debate has been about everything except Syria. About our credibility, at the beginning, about respect for rules and red lines, about America's role in the world, about unipolarity and multipolarity, and about the twilight of the United Nations. About humanitarian intervention, Kosovo, Bosnia, ethics, and realism. Ethics and cynicism. Then the English Parliament turned Cameron down. And it was time to analyze relations between the United States and Great Britain. And France, what will France do? Will it take advantage of Britain's withdrawal to recoup an international role? And Europe, does it exist? And the Arab countries, of course, the Gulf and the price of oil. And then Obama decided to consult Congress and the debate focused on him, not on Syria. A weak president, a strong president, a president who uses strong words, an undeserved Nobel, Republicans and conservatives, the trauma of Iraq. Is he a hawk or a dove? Or simply confused? Guantanamo, drones, and maybe he'd be better off concentrating on the debt and the economy. And so on, up until the recent Russian initiative for destroying Assad's chemical arsenal. And now it's all about analyzing relations between the U.S. and Russia, and Putin's return, and Iran—how does all this affect Iran's nuclear capability? Which is the only thing of real interest, because, as usual, who knows the consequences for Israel? Actually we've talked about everything these days except possible solutions. Negotiations, transitions. And we asked everyone for an opinion. Except the Syrians.

And so the debate says little about Syria, but a lot about us. Because in point of fact, once we'd gotten over the shock of the images of the chemical attack, once we began to think clearly, there was nearly unanimous consensus on the uselessness of retaliation. For differing reasons. Some in support of negotiations, others in favor of a more incisive intervention with ground troops. In any case, the idea of two days of missiles seemed senseless to many. The war, they kept repeating, will go on as before. Moreover, the repercussions on neighboring countries would be unpredictable. Yet, when Obama stopped the countdown and decided to consult Congress, the criticism of a ineffectual hawk turned into criticism of a reluctant hawk. It's surprising, isn't it? No one denies that intervening in Syria is a complex and controversial decision, yet we object to the fact that Obama decided to listen, to think. To reflect. We object to the fact that he allows himself to be influenced by the opinions of the American people. Like that ingenuous Cameron—didn't he know that voters are against the war because they are self-seeking? Because they don't understand what's in the true national interest? Didn't he know that if it were up to them, we would never have landed in Normandy? We question democracy.

We question what is basically our goal in Syria.

We want a self-confident leader, a commander who projects muscle and testosterone; we want a hero who acts, and acts quickly, even though we've just warned him that it's hopeless, and even risky, to act solely for the sake of acting. Cheering from the stands now passes for debate, social networks are our parliament: today, this is what we mean by democracy.

But, most importantly, why have we decided that no diplomatic solutions exist for Syria? For a mediator, the most thorny standing case is Israel and Palestine: two protagonists, one subordinate to the other, one ensnared by the other, left alone at the negotiating table with their imbalance of resources and power. But a plurality of protagonists and interests, as we have in Syria, always results in a meeting of interests, as well as differences—opportunities, as well as obstacles. "The only reason to support Assad is if you consider the alternative to be worse. If you think Assad, though criminal, is less criminal than the rebels. And vice versa: those who side with the rebels now side with the rebels only because they are against the regime." I could delete the quotation marks; it's what they all tell you in Syria. No one can lose, but no one can win. And yet, they also say, this is exactly why there's room for compromise.

For peace.

If only we listened to the Syrians at times.

If only we cared about what the Syrians had to say, we could now avoid days of debate on the Russian initiative. And not just because they've been neutralizing chemical weapons for twenty years now in Iraq. "What do I think of all this?" asks Mohammed Noor, making a long story short. "That more than 110,000 Syrians have been killed by conventional weapons. Eighty times the number of gas victims."

AND NOW THAT it's official, they've all left.

Now that Obama has made up his mind. No bombing.

And they all left.

On the other hand, in Cairo the activists end up back in prison. Clashes, attacks. And everywhere hangs the portrait of General al-Sisi, the man responsible for the coup. Like the portrait of Mubarak before. "What, you're still in Ramallah?" Lorenzo asked me. "Don't tell me you're going to miss Egypt."

It seems normal now, Syria, the war.

And the journalists are gone.

"There's nothing to write about."

The first photo always arrives around 5 a.m. Today's shot is a courtyard with red, blue, and green patches scattered about. Clothing. An Islamic charity that distributed clothes. At night, to prevent being seen. But they were struck by a mortar. Almost all of the victims were children, sent to preclude being hit. Because you think: Children. Let's send the children, children won't be targeted. If you enlarge the photo, zoom in, some of the tattered rags aren't rags at all. Meaning, they're not cloth.

Then comes a photo of some children reflected in a pool of blood. A missile strike—a picture of rescue workers after the missile, digging through stone after stone with their bare hands. An eleven-story building. A photo of fathers carrying their children in their arms, lined up as if at the entrance to a nursery, but instead they're in line at a cemetery, their children wrapped in white cloth. A little boy on a bike pedaling swiftly past the snipers, head down, and this little girl with a flower in her hair, a pleated skirt, collecting scraps of metal to make weapons. "Come play with me?" she asks, with her flower in her hair, and another little boy nearby is missing an arm and is playing in front of the ruins of al-Shifa. They're playing at being executed against a wall, they are playing at being tortured, they are playing at being corpses, at being mutilated, this head wedged in the rubble, charred. "Come play with me?" she asks while everything, all around, explodes, explodes and topples, blood drips on them as they skin a rat, emaciated, yellow from typhus, skin and bones and scars. "Come play with me?" as they search for a corpse, search for food, or fly on swings soaring over common graves. You walk along and they cling to your arm, follow you, as if you were worthy, as if you were here to save them, collecting all the fingers they can find, a bouquet of fingers of the field, as if you were worthy and everywhere you turn, those heads, they stare at you, those heads among the rubble, that questioning look, they stare at you, the blood dripping down, they stare at you as if to say: I don't understand those feet, those hands, those arms in the rubble, and they cling to you as you run away, asking, "Come play with me?" these charred children, these empty eye sockets, "Come play with me?" and they pull you down, they grab you, as if you were there to save them, they grip you by the ankles and . . .

IT'S 3:37 IN THE MORNING.
   Only 3:37.
   I keep waking up at the same time.
   But all that's left are the photographs.
   None of us is willing to go to Syria anymore.
   Even Father Paolo Dall'Oglio has disappeared. He'd lived in Syria for thirty years at the monastery of Mar Musa, not far from Damascus, and was—still *is*—the symbol of dialogue between Christianity and Islam in Syria. He had returned a few days ago, after being expelled by Assad. And he was headed to Raqqa, the only city controlled by the rebels, and

therefore the first city of democratic Syria. A tenacious opponent of the regime, he had returned to start again.

But he was kidnapped by Al Qaeda.

Even Father Paolo Dall'Oglio.

Kidnapped by the rebels.

An opponent of the regime.

So now none of us reporters dares to return.

What's left are the photographs.

The emails. "Obama thinks about bombing and suddenly
you're all prepared to take a chance. Because for you the news
isn't the war in Syria, it's American foreign policy. You your-
selves are the news. For you being for or against bombing
means being for or against the United States. For you journalists, there's nothing to write about, apart from the United
States, apart from all of you," a Syrian wrote to me. He said,
"Shame on you."

Only these kinds of messages are left.

Hour after hour.

Minute after minute. They're killing us all! Where are you?
They're killing us all!

Only these emails.

And photos of blood.

I TRIED REWORKING my list. But it still says R for Red, C for
Corpse, A for Airplane, H for Helicopter, E for Explodes. R
for Rubble.

R for Rubble, M for Mortars, W for Wounded, B for Blade,
G for Grief. G for Guilt.

O for Obsession.

"Change jobs!" Elias yelled at me yesterday. I had phoned

him to see if anyone felt like going back to Aleppo. "What more do you want from Syria? Forget the war!" he shouted. "Forget about Syria! If you're not able to forget, if you're not able to move on, do something else! Write novels! You and your Syria! Write a novel. This is no job for people who are fragile! What do you expect from Syria?" he yelled at me. And he hung up. Just like that.

He's one of the best. A photographer who has portrayed Syria as few others have.

But now we don't even talk about it among ourselves. I mean, we thirty-somethings who were there at al-Shifa. Rooted to the spot. So we wouldn't miss the bombings, because we knew it was only a matter of time. Only a matter of aim. We knew that some of us would be killed, yet we stayed there. Tacitly taking turns in shifts. Especially the photographers.

Italians, Spaniards. The ones who in Italy we call *bamboccioni*, stay-at-homers who still live with their parents.

But now we don't even talk about it, our own ghosts.

Each of us who can't sleep. Though no one will say it.

Each of us talking in our sleep about brutality and carnage.

Especially after it became a war. After everything changed, after everything went bad, and you are no longer the same person the activists helped get across the border illegally. Because everyone sees you as nothing more than an instrument: an instrument of propaganda or an instrument of profit. Everyone: the rebels, the regime, and everyone around you, who in reality have zero interest in Syria, in the world. In you. They're all there waiting for your photo, your piece. An icon. While all you have are children grasping at your ankles.

Because the hardest thing, in the end, isn't writing about the front, about other people's wars, but your own. And so here we are. Each with his own ghosts.

Here, where we don't even talk about it anymore.

If you're unable to move on.

If you can't forget.

O for Obsession.

But who is more rational? Those who move on or those who stay put? Those who observe or those who deny? Those who aren't traumatized by 110,000 deaths, by two years of war? Who is more rational?

More fragile? Those who look or those who look away?

Because in the end you can hide all you want, but it's like those portraits by the Dutch photographer Claire Felicie, like those marines before and after Afghanistan. When only a year had passed, and instead it seemed like ten: the rough skin and that unreadable expression, as though they'd been scorched by life. Like the photos in our passports, if we look through them. If we confront ourselves: Before. After.

Elsewhere. Endlessly elsewhere, as I wander through Ramallah, through this city that was the beacon of the Middle East. No longer my home.

"Change jobs!"

"What more do you want from Syria?"

"See a shrink."

I look at Alessio's photos.

Once, twice, a hundred times. Just Alessio's photos.

Radiohead's music.

Nothing but Alessio's photos.

Because there's a story.

And it's not over. F for Fragile, F for Fear. P for Passion.

In the newsroom they reassure me: "You can write about Syria just as well from Rome."

Or from Ramallah.

There's no need to go back.

SURE. BAD ENOUGH you have no idea what's happening in Syria even when you're in Syria.

Those looks boring into you.

Heads in the rubble.

All I know is there's a story there.

It's not over.

A for Angels. D for Demons.

Kill my demons, and you kill my angels.

L for Loneliness.

S for Syria. M for Mirror.

But what does it matter? You can write about Syria just as well from Rome.

Because, though you don't realize it, the only ones left who are still writing about Syria are Syrians. They work for the major agencies, the major newspapers, and contribute with articles written from New York, Paris, London. They are the famous "citizen journalists," highly glorified even by those who would never think of going to a "citizen dentist." The result is cases like that of Elizabeth O'Bagy, the analyst at an American research institute who was cited by John Kerry at the time of the chemical attack. The *Wall Street Journal*, in fact, had just published one of her pieces about the rebels, which essentially gave the impression that they are decent people, and that there are only a handful of extremists in Syria. Because for the U.S., that is the problem, isn't it? They are afraid that Assad could be replaced by Al Qaeda. Shortly afterward, while Human Rights Watch denounced the rebels for crimes against humanity, it was discovered that not only did Elizabeth O'Bagy not have a PhD as she had claimed, but more importantly that she was on the payroll of a Syrian lobby whose objective was to persuade Obama to intervene. In the age of Twitter and YouTube, when newspapers save on correspondents because they can always find some Syrian on Skype who will recap what took place in front of his house, we base our foreign policy on reports like those by Elizabeth O'Bagy. Our wars.

The resulting deaths.

On the reports of a person who began to write about the Middle East two years ago and who was born in 1987.

What does it matter? You can write about Syria just as well from Rome.

AUTUMN 2013

In line at the gate for Antakya, standing in front of me at the Istanbul airport, are two guys with beards, Korans, and British passports. One is missing an arm. The other an ear.

I'm not the only one returning to Aleppo.

But only jihadists remain now. There's no media left in Antakya. The TV networks, the BBC, Sky, still have their offices there, all their equipment, but no one to man it, just a few local staff. Correspondents from newspapers like the *Guardian*, *Le Monde*, correspondents from real newspapers who cover the entire Middle East, don't have a free minute now that everything is in upheaval, so they swing by every two or three months.

The others weren't there before, and aren't there now.

We freelancers aren't there anymore either.

"There's nothing to report," a Spanish guy who came to pick up his bulletproof jacket immediately tells me. "It's pointless. They're where they were a year ago."

Even the Ozsut is deserted.

I ask for an espresso. "Sorry, we don't have any," they tell me. "Only Turkish coffee."

The only ones left are jihadists and NGO people. The way they are now, it's as if they weren't there. The great majority are young people living as if they were someplace else, a place that is identical throughout the world, with their banana cakes and evenings for foreigners only, unmistakably all dressed alike, hanging out only with each other, getting drunk in countries where alcohol is forbidden, and things like that. Like in Ramallah on New Year's Eve, who can forget it? New Year's Eve 2009, when the Danes threw a party on a terrace and meanwhile Gaza was an inferno.

Because those were the days of Operation Cast Lead.

Nearly 1,400 deaths, all of Ramallah in the dark as a show of solidarity, all of Ramallah silent, and that festively illuminated terrace. The music blaring.

By now you can expect anything from the NGOs.

Not that operating here is easy. The first obstacle is Assad, of course, who allows only a few friendly NGOs to operate in Syrian territory. The second obstacle is Turkey, which initially handled everything itself through its primary NGO ascribable to Prime Minister Erdogan. Because for Erdogan it's not a question of solidarity: Syria is an opportunity to show the world what Turkey is capable of—this Turkey that the European Union rejected. But then the number of refugees rose to tens of thousands in just a few months, an unsustainable financial burden, triggering a crisis and threatening to drag Turkey down with it. And so our NGOs obtained the first authorizations. Though with a thousand hurdles and constraints, and strict controls, for fear that now that they've arrived they'll start dealing with other things—with the Kurds, for example. For sure, operating here isn't easy.

Especially given the third obstacle, the war.

"But the problem is that the NGOs have hung back at the border for a year. Now it's dangerous, true, but they didn't go in even when it was possible," Mahmoud Saeed from the Media Center in Aleppo tells me. "Many were afraid of the mortars. Which is more than understandable. But if you're afraid of mortars, which is the least that can be dropped on you in a war, don't raise funds saying that you'll distribute aid in war zones. Explain that you will distribute your blankets to those who manage to flee and reach Turkey on their own, while the rest are dying, starving to death. Because when you promote yourself as a hero, people then think we have humanitarian aid, that someone is doing something, that you're here. In Aleppo, we've never seen a single bottle of water, not one bag of rice, with the logo of one of your NGOs."

Of the dozens of NGOs lingering at the border, only Doctors Without Borders, after months of negotiations, months of persistence, set up its hospitals. One of them was the infirmary where they treated my knee. God only knows how brave, how generous they were there, because it was like al-Shifa, with bombings twice a week on average, in a city so small that everyone knew it was only a matter of time. A matter of aim.

Yet they were there.

Because the point—the point is that, unlike others, some do go in. People in Need, for example. A small NGO from the Czech Republic. When none of the others went, with their Master's degrees and doctorates in humanitarian crises, their years spent testing procedures, calculating the right algorithm for distributing blankets, the universal algorithm, when the others didn't go, Michal Przedlacki did. A man of few words, thirty-four years old, with very pale blue eyes, in

jeans, T-shirt, and scarf. He was in Thailand, the day of the
tsunami, when it seemed like everyone around him died.

And instead of going home, back to his advertising agency,
he went to Chechnya.

In all these months, he's been the only foreigner living in
Aleppo. And when you ask him how it happened, all he says,
shyly, is "commitment." Commitment and passion.

"I'm not here for others. There's no such thing as *their* life
and *my* life—this is *our* life. And when you're here, and the
Syrians understand that you're trying, that maybe you won't
succeed in the end, but that you're trying, day by day, as hard
as you can, and that you're sharing their lives—it's not as if
you come in for ten minutes, throw them a couple of sacks
of potatoes and rush off. You're settled here, you live here.
When they realize that you know what it means to be here, a
social protective net forms around you. Which is, after all, the
only real protection in situations like this. Everyone thinks it's
about dollars. Dollars and strength, like in the movies, paying
the best-equipped guards, the toughest rebels. But there are
things you can't buy. For example, respect. It's the opposite:
you have to fit in. You have to build human relationships, not
contractual ones. You have to stay here because you care, not
just because it's your job. If you do that, it doesn't mean you're
invulnerable. It's not to say it's easy. But you can try."

No, it isn't easy. For months now, Michal hasn't slept.

For months I have woken up at the same hour.

"Everyone asks me why. Why do you stay there? But, simply
put, once you've seen, you can't unsee. Once you've seen, as
Arundhati Roy says, remaining silent becomes as much a
political act as speaking out. As acting. Either way, whatever
you choose to do, you're accountable. I'm not the only one

who stays: in a way, we're all here. Those who keep silent and those who don't. Those who look or those who look away. We're all here. Each of us can decide which side to take."

In fact, there are others who would like to try. Including an extraordinary Italian woman. But she is so frustrated by having spent months here without ever going in, writing and rewriting reports about a Syria she's never seen, that she has decided to drop everything and study nursing. As an American aid worker says: "I tell my boss about Michal, and my boss, from Washington, says to me: 'That guy is one of those who do what the Syrians tell him. They tell him they need rice and he buys them rice. And maybe they need sugar more than rice.' Humanitarian aid has its own rules," he says. "It's not improvisation. You have to follow the rules." Then he tells me: "Only sometimes you have to follow your conscience too. Play by the rules, but also go by what's real."

And there are others like him. A German aid worker. Another American. Disheartened. Stuck in their offices in Antakya, planning what Syria needs without ever having been in Syria.

Distributing blankets to refugees, but only to those who manage to flee on their own.

And yet the vast majority aren't bothered by it. They hang around here, bored, between one meeting and another. They plan outings and get together for drinks. They are already excited about Halloween. They are keeping an eye out for typhoons and earthquakes because they've discovered that Antakya doesn't even have a movie theater or a real disco, nothing, and the girls here don't have sex before marriage. They want to leave. They know Syria as much as they know Antarctica. "I have several contacts with Hezbollah who might help you," a Frenchman who's been in Lebanon kindly tells me. He leaves me a slip of paper with some phone numbers. Hezbollah. Sure. They could help me disappear. Hezbollah is with Assad. Or this other Frenchman who deals with minorities, flour and minorities, and calls me because he's looking for a representative from every Christian community. He has to deliver his flour. He calls me and says: "Do you think you can find me some Copts? I have an Orthodox and a Chaldean. I even have a Melkite, an Assyrian too," he tells me, "but I'm missing the Copts." It's not that he's missing them; it's that they're missing in Syria because they're found in Egypt.

It's confidential. You ask them what they're distributing, where, and they tell you: *It's confidential.* How they choose the areas in which to operate, which areas have the most urgent needs, how many people they assist—ask them anything. Ask them what the weather is like and they tell you: *It's confidential.*

All they'll tell you is that they distribute aid through Syrian NGOs. For anything else, they tell you to call their press office in London or Brussels. And the press office tells you that it's all online. Online, at best you learn that they have a budget of "X million euros." Not a word about how the money is used. With what results. Apart from what the Syrians say: "We're starving."

But there are small exceptions. The Czechs. And the Norwegians, as usual, go anywhere.

"About a dozen NGOs are ready to step in. But no one contacts us. And when we asked that milk for babies be made a priority in Aleppo, they said it was a cultural matter, that breast milk is better than powdered milk. And they suggested we do a training session for women," Mohammed says. Who in April was wearing a Metallica sweatshirt, working for a Western NGO. Now he has a beard and works for a charity linked to Al Qaeda.

I have no doubt that it is less black and white than that. And this is Aleppo: only Aleppo. Maybe farther east, farther south, it's different in Uganda. But for the moment, this is all they tell me—all I can write about. There are two pieces that are impossible to write here. A piece on the Islamists. And a piece on humanitarian aid. It's hopeless: they don't speak to journalists. But Al Qaeda's salaries are not paid with our donations.

It's confidential.

That's all I'm allowed to write.

Too dangerous to go in, they say.

The only way is to rely directly on the Syrians, they tell you.

On the other hand, the National Coalition even has an internal Assistance Coordination Unit specializing in humanitarian aid and reconstruction. It was established a little less than a year ago, in December 2012, and has raised forty-seven million dollars to date. The bills are kept in packets in a storeroom. But here, too, it's hopeless; they don't speak to journalists. The only ones who explained the results obtained were two officials, Bassam al-Kuwatly and Mohammed Ayoub. After they resigned. "The money was delivered in plastic bags. Someone would say: 'I need $150,000 for this project.' And he was given $150,000. Without a shred of paper to justify that the $150,000 was actually needed. And above all, that the project was needed."

Disproportionate salaries, incompetence, unjustified expenses. Mark Ward, an American diplomat, commented: "Better than nothing." At first, the group whose phone line functioned the best received the money.

Later a shy, introverted man who had been a laborer all his life would manage to accomplish what the National Coalition never could, what neither the UN nor the NGOs nor anyone else could do—those like me, who spent years studying for a degree in solidarity, then a Master's in refugees, and another degree in locusts and famines. Yakzan Shishakly, thirty-six years old, was born in Damascus, and after finishing high school he immigrated to Houston, Texas, where he paid for courses in English by working as a waiter, and he started a company that installed air conditioners. When in September 2012 he saw the war rapidly advance, along with the world's indifference, he came back here. At the border, behind barbed wire, he saw women and children, in the rain out in the open, with nothing. The border sealed. And he simply asked them what they needed most. They told him tents, and that's how he started. With what he had in his pocket. Today thirty thousand people live in his camp at Atmeh. For each family, he spends eight times less than what the United Nations spends on refugees a few miles away.

Of course, Yakzan Shishakly isn't fond of journalists either. When you approach with your notebook, he points to the refugees and tells you: "Don't write about me. They're the story, not me."

He tells you, "Do what you can with those few lines you have.

"Even if it is just a few lines," he says, "even if they do not seem like much, they are important."

He says: "They are your part."

Yakzan, in Arabic, means "he who is awake." He who is aware.

Who has a conscience.

Because there is no one left here.

It's too dangerous.

And besides—why risk it? After all, you can write about Syria just as well from Rome, can't you?

On Twitter, on Facebook, on YouTube. Even though the news and even the images aren't verifiable. Nor current. The first star of the Syrian Spring, in 2011, was a gay activist from Damascus followed by half the world. Amina. Until the *Guardian* realized that her name was Tom MacMaster and that he was writing from Edinburgh. Or the photo that moved everyone the other day: a child sleeping between his parents' graves. Except it had been taken in Saudi Arabia as part of an artistic performance.

Everyone keeps saying: What are you doing there?

Why don't you go to Cairo?

"Read this analysis from the front!" the U.S. State Department tweeted excitedly yesterday. It was a piece by a young repoter already quoted by the *Washington Post* and the *Economist* as an expert on Islamic militant groups, and in particular on jihad in Syria.

Then a reporter called him for an interview.

He's twenty-one years old and studied literature at Oxford. He's never been to Syria.

Because by now there's this idea, right? That if something exists, it's on the Internet. And vice versa. If it's not on the Internet, it doesn't exist. But if it really happened, if it's true, it's on the Internet.

It's just a matter of digging around and finding it.

And if it's on the Internet, if it's just a matter of digging around and finding it, why stay here?

Go home.

The danger.

What do you still want with Syria?

The problem is that the definition may be new, but the phenomenon isn't new. Because "citizen journalists" in fact fall into two categories. The individual who is there by chance, on September 11, for example, walking his dog near the Twin Towers. He takes a picture with his phone and describes one of the planes crashing. But we already have a word for him: eyewitness. And no one would ever think of asking him to do an analysis of Al Qaeda, on which to then base the decision to bomb Afghanistan. In the second category are those who live in Aleppo under a regime, rather than in Havana, or in Taranto, in the shadow of the ILVA steelworks, who take pictures every day, report the devastation day by day, constantly. Who document. Invaluable. Especially in Syria, with so many cities inaccessible. However we already have a word for them as well. They're called activists. And like all activists, not only do some merely defend their own cause, their own interests, their view of things; on the contrary, that's their job. But even the more moderate ones are simply too involved. Journalism is a question of detachment: a matter of being at the right distance. Not too close, not too far away. Any journalist knows that at some point he has to go, especially at the very moment when he's become a so-called expert and everyone seeks him out. He has to go, because he's too close to it by now, because a lot of things now seem normal to him. They've become invisible to him.

Because he starts to say, "There's nothing to write about."

Every journalist knows this.

That information is one thing, journalism another.

That journalism is what is constructed based on information.

But we all seem to have forgotten that here.

When a year ago, in the streets of Aleppo, we ran into the first victims who'd been tortured by the rebels, dragged by the hair, all bloodied, I still remember Giulio wanting to take a picture. Naturally, the rebels kept him at a distance. "What happened?" I asked.

"He fell down the stairs."

Like in the emergency room, right? When a wife arrives. A girlfriend.

She fell down the stairs.

The question is always the same. What are you doing in Antakya?

It's all online.

What are you still doing there? It's all on YouTube.

Call the rebels, they'll tell you about it. They'll even send you photos, you know?

Every day.

Thirty times. What the hell are you still doing there?

Still, Syria is remote, even when you're in Syria.

Aleppo, too, is remote, even when you're in Aleppo. When you're at the front, you have to call Rome in the evening, so that someone can read you the news agencies' reports and recap what's happened, meanwhile, around you. Because all you know is what occurred in your corner of the old city, there with a lone cat and a couple of snipers. Especially in the other half of Aleppo. The part that's under the control of the regime. Which is a hundred yards in front of us. I've been here for two years now and I still don't know what's going on across the river. What life is like there. It's off limits even to journalists who have a visa. Some talk about cafés, restaurants. Shops open for business. Normal things. Schools, offices. They say there's asphalt across the river, street lights, and paved roads. That there's water. Others, however, tell of displaced persons, thousands of displaced families. They tell of snipers and mortars, mortars fired by the rebels. As undiscriminating as those of the regime.

They report everything and its opposite.

And we will never know the truth.

Even if it's all online. All on YouTube.

Because the truth is that even in Aleppo we have no idea what's happening in Aleppo.

Yet the question is always the same. What are you still doing there?

There's nothing to write about.

They're where they were a year ago. "Go to Cairo."

"Go to the Central African Republic."

"But I don't know anything about the Central African Republic."

"Exactly. No one even knows where it is. You can write whatever you want."

"Still going on about Syria!" Lorenzo says sharply, he too having come to pick up his bulletproof jacket and assorted equipment. "What is it with you, an obsession? They'll end up kidnapping you, and Italy will have to pay your ransom with my taxes! Instead of funding nursery schools," he says, his voice rising. "We have to bankroll your obsession! And then we won't have nursery schools! Because of paying ransoms for people like you! Do you hear that?" he yells to the guy at the nearby table. "They go to Syria to be kidnapped, and then I have to pay their ransom! And for what? What? To report that the Syrians are where they were a year ago! Because they're obsessed! Go see a shrink," he tells me. And he stalks out.

Then he comes back. "This is no job for a woman!" And he walks out again.

Everybody in the Ozsut is watching us.

And anyway, Lorenzo has never paid any taxes. Because almost all of them have a foreign account, in Lebanon, for instance, countries like that. And an account in Italy for the small change.

It's one of the most popular topics of conversation here. How to evade taxes.

Still, it's true that the Syrians are where they were a year ago.

Yes. Except the rebels are crumbling.

And everything is changing.

Even if things are where they were a year ago.

In the beginning, the rebels were defending their neighborhoods, the blocks where they lived. That's how it started, and often it's still that way. Scattered groups who only have scarce funds that trickle in from abroad, typically from Syrians originally from the same areas. You meet these rebels everywhere, busy crafting their handmade weapons from leftover sheet metal, street posts. Rusty cans. You meet them as they aim left to flush out a sniper on their right, as grenades explode in their hands. Sometimes the journalists happen to be the more experienced ones at the front; sometimes they have to explain how to use a mortar. And the rebels don't ask for more ammunition these days, but for food: they're hungry.

In addition to the young guys with Kalashnikovs and flip-flops, others have banded together in larger, better-equipped groups. Such as the Liwa al-Tawhid, the Unity Brigade, the toughest in Aleppo. Or the Ahrar al-Sham, the Free Men of the Levant, which is the largest moderate Islamic brigade and also has a section for humanitarian aid. The assassination of its leader a few days ago, the work of Al Qaeda, triggered the clashes now underway. Unlike the more radical jihadists who are outside of the Free Army, groups such as Ahrar al-Sham claim a greater sphere for sharia, but in the context of a secular, plural Syria. It's difficult to get to the truth, however; they don't speak to journalists. "If you have questions, you can find everything on our Facebook page," they say. Not the best advice. The first thing you find on Google are videos of heads chopped off. The most recent one, in Aleppo, in a hospital: a patient groggy from anesthesia was murmuring Shiite verses. Only when he was already decapitated did they realize that he was one of them.

The problem is that what we call the Free Army is not synonymous, generally speaking, with the resistance. It has never included all the insurgents, nor has it ever been able to coordinate them or identify priorities, to formulate a strategy. For a variety of reasons. The first and foremost is that it has long been led by Turkey. By general Riad al-Assad, known for giving orders via Skype. But above all, the Free Army is undermined by competition between Saudi Arabia and Qatar, who vie for the loyalty of the various brigades with rounds of cash. And with individual autonomous brigades seeking and managing arms and resources, the result is that there is no chain of command, and crimes and abuses go unpunished. And it's not just looting: Abu Sakkar, the rebel who feasted on the heart of a loyalist, was never removed from duty.

The problem is that what we call the Free Army doesn't exist. A few days ago, thirteen brigades—about 80 percent of the rebels—split off from the National Coalition. They don't intend to recognize a government in exile, they have stated, but plan to create a Syria based on sharia. In part because, to be completely honest, rechristening themselves Islamists is the easiest way to rake in dollars from wealthy charities in the Gulf nations. With $175 you can adopt a child long-distance, for life, or donate fifty bullets for a sniper in Syria; $400 and you buy him eight mortar rounds.

DEVASTATED BY hunger and epidemics, decimated by missiles, Syrians are disconcerted to see the Free Army wrangle with the National Coalition, and besides that, even more seriously, clash with the Islamists. In fact, each time you come back here you find that the former *bad guys* are now the *good guys*, because players have emerged who are even more extremist. And just as Ahrar al-Sham, which terrorized us a year ago, then started protecting us from Jabhat al-Nusra, the group that introduced suicide bombings, today it is Jabhat al-Nusra that protects us from ISIS, the Islamic State of Iraq and the Levant, the off-shoot of Al Qaeda founded in 2004 in Iraq to eradicate not only the Americans, but also the Shiites. Its aim is not to over-throw Assad, but to capture parts of Syria and restore the caliphate. They are all foreigners. And their number grew with the attack on the Abu Ghraib prison in Baghdad, in July 2013, when hundreds of them who had been detained there promptly flocked here. They were also bolstered by the removal of Morsi in Egypt, which was interpreted as evidence that it's useless to win power through elections, because the U.S. will then orga-nize a coup. Evidence that the only way is jihad.

Because the Middle East, at times, isn't complicated.

And so, these days the rebels are all united in the war against ISIS, which for now is in control and commands the border crossings, namely, the critical supply routes from Turkey. Reports from the checkpoints are unvarying: summary executions of anyone deemed to be an infidel. Names are now circulating for the first time. The first stories were told in a low voice. Deserters who decided to desert again.

Who decided to go back to Assad.

Because it's true: they are where they were a year ago.

Except things are no longer the same.

And yet everyone will tell you there's nothing to write about.

Only Narciso Contreras is still here. He won the Pulitzer with his photos and yet he's still here. Aleppo is off limits now, too many Al Qaeda checkpoints. But he's still here, going wherever else it's possible to go in Syria. He returned to us last night.

But it's tough. He says, "The newspapers aren't interested."

Even though readers write to you. They write to you because they want to know:

"Really, these chemical weapons, how many are there?"

"And what's going on in Egypt? We don't know anything anymore!"

"And Libya, what's happening now in Libya? Who's in government?"

"Why isn't there a line or two on Pakistan? Is the story about the drones true?"

"And chemical weapons, what's the situation? Why don't we know anything anymore?"

Dozens of emails like that.

Every day. All these notes from readers. All wanting to know.

And messages from Syrians. In desperate refrain: "They're killing us all! Where are you? They're killing us all!"

Only our readers and the Syrians. Otherwise, it's always the same:

"Call the rebels, okay? They'll tell you about it. And anyway, it's all on YouTube. What are you doing still there? There's nothing to write about. There's nothing to report, get it? Nothing. Nothing, don't you understand? There's nothing to report, what do you still want with Syria? They're where they were a year ago, get it? Don't you see?"

Nothing.

And so I stay at home in the evening. I read, study.

I look at Alessio's photos.

No one calls me. Then again, friends in Italy are at the end of their rope, drained by the crisis. All unemployed or with a contract about to expire, all going through a bad time, all with degrees and no work, no rights: no future. Disheartened.

Scattered far and wide. They reply, "Sorry, but I don't feel like talking. I feel like a worthless loser."

All lost and crushed.

Sorry, they say. "Syria is all I need tonight. All I need are the world's problems." And it's true: nearly forty years old, a doctorate, and you can't afford to pay a dentist. There's Anna with a young son, a husband whose contract wasn't renewed on Tuesday, five months of salary in arrears, and a boss, meanwhile, who drives around in a Porsche and says there's a crisis, we all have to make sacrifices. And here I am with my Syria, with my wars. What can I expect? They, too, are at war.

Defeated.

While the editors, as usual, are waiting for a piece ASAP, and the rest doesn't seem to concern them. All they say: "Let us know when you come back from Aleppo."

When I come back. Sure.

If I come back.

And so I stay home in the evening. Looking through Alessio's photos.

And wondering what's the point.

I think about my old prof, Cassese. Who would have sought justice.

I think about international law, about my old life.

While I'm here looking for a way to get into Aleppo rather than a way to drag Assad to The Hague. Because anything I may write, no matter how good, whatever life I may risk, this war and every war will go on. Cassese would have tried to stop it. He would never have settled for reporting on it.

It's not as if I'm the BBC. As if I can change anything.

Here I am with all my energies focused on a way to get into Aleppo.

All my energies wasted here, wondering what's the point.

I'm thinking about Cassese. And I miss him.

I only know that I miss him, sitting here, thinking I have made a mess of everything.

And still I keep looking at those photos.

Once, twice, a hundred times.

Those eyes. It's been two years now, but they nail you every time.

Every time. You think you're looking at them, and instead they're looking at you.

There's a story and it's not over.

That day at al-Shifa. That doctor. When he told me: "Don't write that everything is at a standstill, that there is no progress. The dead are making progress." And what he had in his hand: bloody bits of skull I thought were plaster.

He too is now dead.

The only one who calls me is Daniel. Daniel Bettini, foreign bureau chief at *Yedioth Ahronoth*. The leading Israeli news-paper. "I'm sorry," I told him, "I'm really focused on Syria, you know?" I would have liked to write about all the changes taking place between the Israelis and the Palestinians—because everything is changing between them, even if they are where they were forty years ago. I would have liked to write about a thousand other things these past few months. I said, "I'm sorry." He told me that writing about Syria, about people under siege, starving, forgotten by the world, writing about Syria today "is the most Jewish thing you can do." He said, "You're a Jew, when you're in Aleppo."

And so he calls me. All the time.

And then Mustafa Barghouti. I worked for him a few years ago. He's a doctor. A doctor and a deputy, one of the leaders of nonviolent resistance to Israeli occupation. But also of resis-tance to Hamas and Fatah, since for the Palestinians, by now, they are as much an obstacle to freedom as the Wall. We had an idea of doing a book together. But while I was in Ramallah, my head was in Aleppo. "I'm sorry," I told him, too. I would have liked to do a thousand other things these past months. He told me that writing about Syria, about people under siege, starving, forgotten by the world, writing about Syria today "is the most Palestinian thing you can do."

I looked at Alessio's photos one last time.

I don't even know where he is.

But I'm sure he doesn't sleep. That at night, he talks of bloodshed and fighting.

Because there's a story in them. It's no use. Once you've seen.

And you can't unsee.

"DON'T WORRY," Ahmed tells me, as we cross the last check-point and enter the city, as a mortar strike makes the air shudder. "Now that you're in Aleppo, you're safe."

And he ducks his head to dodge a sniper.

My first time here, a little over a year ago, I wasn't even wearing the veil under my helmet. Then, after the veil, one day they asked me to wear a long pullover. After the long pull-over, a garment down to my ankles. And now even a wedding ring on my finger—"Because you must always walk beside a man, the man to whom you belong." And now that the Isla-mists are in control, and the priority for many is not Assad but sharia, now that the rebels' crimes have been added to the regime's crimes, and journalists are forbidden to enter—cur-rently, eighteen of us are missing without a trace—today my helmet is a veil. My bulletproof jacket is a *nijab*. Because the only way to slip into Aleppo is to pass for a Syrian woman. Disguised. No questions on the street, not even a notebook, a pen. "But it's not really a matter of the veil," a woman tells me, having recognized me immediately by my skin, by my hands. "To look like a Syrian today you have to be filthy, haggard, and desperate."

Aleppo is nothing today but hunger and Islam. Kids play on swings in the narrowest alleyways to avoid the mortars—boys on the right holding their plastic Kalashnikovs, girls on the left already veiled, while a couple of jihadist fathers car-ingly push.

About one million Syrians still live here in Aleppo under the control of the Free Army. They never had the $150 to pay for a car to the Turkish border. Dozens of children, barefoot, ragged, and disfigured by the scars of leishmaniasis, tag after emaciated mothers, also barefoot and completely in black, fully covered, all with bowl in hand, in search of a mosque where bread is distributed, yellow with typhus. And their eyes bore into you when you meet them, like all genuine children of war, who are never the ones we show you in newspapers or on television: the ones who smile gratefully when you hand them a biscuit. Because these, in contrast, are real children: exhausted, mute, eyes dazed by the horror of life. We don't show you these children or the children cut down by Assad's missiles, whom you can find pieces of—heads, limbs—in the hospitals.

Meanwhile even the doctors are children now, "Because everyone here has either left or died, and as the world quibbles over fossil fuels, we continue to be killed," says Abu Yazan, twenty-five, a student and impromptu head doctor. Who, he admits, not only has little more than disinfectant and bandages in the supply room; he also has no idea how to treat his patients: "It's one thing to amputate a leg, another to treat ischemia." Aleppo had about five thousand doctors. Today it has thirty-six. Outside the entrance, a tent with a bucket and brush: the only available antidote in case of a chemical attack. And, of course, nameless bodies outside. People pass by, raise the sheet, make sure it's not one of their loved ones.

They're on their own, the Syrians, completely alone, on this side of the red line. Here where you don't die from gas, but from hunger, so nobody cares. 126,000 victims, more than 2 million refugees, 7 million displaced. Almost half the population. Plus the hundreds of thousands under siege—in Homs, in Damascus, everywhere—about whom we know only what little is passed on via Twitter, pictures of skeletons roaming the fields in search of leaves and roots. While state TV was broadcasting the list of concerts in theaters in the center last night, the imam on Al Jazeera was authorizing Syrians to cook stray dogs.

By statute UN aid is distributed through the only recognized government, which is Assad's. Which, however, imposes so many restrictions on movement that a large part of the aid ends up in areas under the control of the regime. The regime claims that it ensures the safety of the humanitarian workers, even though it has arrested and tortured those who have tried to reach areas under rebel control.

And those who managed to reach them were then seized by Al Qaeda.

In theory, Aleppo has a civil administration, the Revolutionary Council. But it was appointed from abroad by the National Coalition, which was created by the international community in opposition to Assad, and whose decisions here are of no interest to anyone. Its delegates have lived in Europe for years—too long. And in any case, only $400,000 arrived, to restore electricity, disinfest the streets of rats, reopen the schools. The hospitals. Forty cents each. It ran out. Lakhdar Brahimi, UN mediator for Syria, earns $189,000 a year.

The only place in Aleppo where you can find a little bread is the mosque.

And so it's no wonder that when I ask to meet with the person in charge, I find myself at the Islamic court. Or rather, disguised, I find myself at the house of Al Qaeda's Luay, his wife's black silhouette knocking at the closed door and leaving the coffee behind it. Every rebel group has its representative in the court. I ask what law they apply and he replies: "Sharia sharia," meaning they don't apply a written code but the will of the judges. "Because in our tradition, the judges are experts in jurisprudence. They are men of authority whom the community trusts." Except that in Aleppo, as usual, everyone is either gone or dead, and so even the judges are children: Luay is thirty-two years old. Before the war he was a practicing attorney. "In fact, it is not easy," he admits. "Everyone has a weapon here and has no need for a court to obtain justice. But above all, it is not easy dealing with the rebels. Looting, extortion. When we attempted to try Nemer, the leader of the more violent militias, his men surrounded the court until we dismissed the case."

The court, in return, issued a ban, duly posted at the entrance to the Karaj al-Hajez checkpoint, the crossing point between the two halves of Aleppo. It looks like a main road, but it's actually something out of a Stephen King novel, controlled by snipers from the three minarets of a mosque. At the checkpoint, the sign says: "Transporting food and medicine is prohibited." Because while at first it was the regime that surrounded and starved the rebels' half of the city, now it's the rebels, having captured all the access roads leading into Aleppo, who surround and starve the regime's half of the city. People tape slices of meat on themselves, fill fake TV sets with eggs. Every now and then, there's an abrupt shot, someone dies. And for half an hour, an hour, the street empties out, the corpse lying there in the sun, a cat sniffing at it. Then the first arrival, a little boy, appears warily from a side street, hesitates a moment, and quickly crosses. A second one, then a third, and the street grows crowded again, the corpse still there. The snipers, in their minarets, wait confidently.

Syrians no longer speak of "liberated areas," but of east Aleppo and west Aleppo. They no longer talk about Assad, injustice, oppression. On their cell phones, they no longer show you pictures of their children or their brothers killed by the regime, but simply beautiful photos of Aleppo before the war. Because no one here is fighting the regime anymore: the rebels are fighting each other.

Those who aren't engaged in looting and extortion are busy opposing ISIS, which now insists on being called only *al-Dawlat*, a.k.a. the State, as if it were a new regime. "We are even less free than before, if such a thing is possible," one of the last activists still here tells me. One of the last still alive. "Because before, unless you were politically engaged, no one interfered in your private affairs. Now everything is forbidden: music, alcohol, cigarettes," he says. "It is not just a matter of Christians and Alawites. Now, all Sunnis who, like me, interpret the Koran differently from Al Qaeda are in danger. Assad targets my life. These people target my lifestyle too."

And yet, he explains, it's a fundamentalism that was imported from abroad. By Islamists, and by Hezbollah, who fight alongside the regime. "You continue to be divided on intervention, not realizing that outside intervention has been going on for months."

People are whispering again in Aleppo, walking with their heads down. In July, Mohammed Kattaa was shot for having inappropriately uttered the name of the Prophet.

He was fifteen years old.

While the front, meanwhile, hasn't budged. In the old city, the first unit of the Free Army in which I was embedded a year ago is still there. Still at the same intersection, still trying to flush out one sniper. A difficult job. Those boys too are hungry. They sold their Kalashnikovs to pay for a wounded comrade to be treated in Turkey. In one day of fighting we advance five blocks. Then the ammunition runs out. And we fall back with seven fewer men.

Because the only real front that still exists here is the sky.

That's how you die, with no warning. An explosion out of nowhere, a lightning flash, a blast of wind and the air in flames, blistering, blood and shrapnel—and in the dust, amid the screams, only these torn shreds of flesh, these charred children. There's no shelter. The houses don't have cellars. Nothing. Still, the only anti-aircraft protection is bad weather. Just like that, you die. You dig with your hands, there are no bulldozers, and in any case there's no fuel, there isn't even electricity. You dig by the light of cell phones, cigarette lighters, the corpses staring at you, packed between remnants of columns.

And for days, at dawn, in silence, on this shoreline of human remains, you see women bent over as if they are searching for seashells. Between their fingers a scrap of cloth, a remnant of a child. Among them, stray dogs with bones between their teeth.

That's how you die, in Aleppo. You die and all that remains of you is a photo in a frame.

Grass has grown among the rubble. War has become this city's skin. Amid the scorched carcasses of cars abandoned, left to hibernate where they swerved, the hole of the bullet that hit the driver through the windshield, wild cyclamen, and a bloodied shirt caught in the wheels. In a barbershop, small glass bottles, intact, are still lined up on the shelves. You uncap them and you can still smell the scent of jasmine. Girls covered to their ankles contemplate shop windows displaying fluorescent, dizzying high heels; in the parks, children chase after a ball between rows of graves while a plane, circling, flies overhead, and it's already been ten minutes now, in a moment it will strike—in a moment someone, one of us, will die. You walk along and a man in front of you suddenly drops: shot down.

Everything now seems routine; nothing is missing, yet nothing is as it should be. In the ambulances you find fighters at the front, children with Kalashnikovs, their fathers killed, everything all haywire. You find the snipers working shifts, arriving at their station for their stint on time, after their morning coffee; they park in front of the door as if they are going to the office. At the rumble of a mortar, children don't even turn. Only when there's a hail of bullets do they begin dickering.

The most symbolic front, in the end, the most indisputable front, is Bustan al-Qasr, because it has long been the epicenter of the Friday demonstrations. The place it all started. And where it all continues, Friday after Friday. Though now the demonstrations are no longer solely against Assad. And at the rally today there are only children. Because everyone is either gone or dead, and those who haven't left or died have disappeared into thin air. Like Abu Maryam. Persecuted by the regime, then by the rebels, he was finally seized by ISIS. And vanished. At the head of the procession is his niece Nasma. Ten years old. The van with the amplifiers still has no gasoline; it's still pushed by hand.

The displaced refugees, however, haven't disappeared; they're still camped not far away, alongside the river. Because for months all its banks have been hollowed out to form burrows. They aren't shacks, they aren't caves, you can't exactly make them out; they're bits and pieces of things, metal sheeting, wooden boards, plastic tarps. Piled up mounds, heaps of pieces of things. At some point you simply find yourself inside, among women, children, maimed and speechless old people, a boy with Down's, on the ground his supper of rice and worms on a scrap of cardboard. Because every time you come back to Aleppo, things are always the same for those displaced: only their names change. Ibtisam Ramdan, twenty-five, used to live here with her three children and tuberculosis in a rank tract of sewer pipe. But she ventured out with the youngest in search of bread, one day, and was hit by a sniper. The other two wasted away in poverty until a mortar pulverized them, in this Aleppo strewn with graves, even in the air, this endless monument to unknown people.

A few yards farther up, the river that divides east Aleppo from west Aleppo continues to spew out the purplish remains of men executed with a bullet to the back of the head, their hands tied. It's never been clear who they are. Rebels executed by the loyalists, or loyalists executed by the rebels. It depends on your point of view—or maybe only on the current.

ON THE SCREEN, the BBC is talking about Moadamiya. It looks like Somalia, with those bodies that are all bones, yet it's only six miles from the center of Damascus, where bankers play tennis at their clubs. Because while the world is focused on chemical attacks, Assad has discovered a more economical method of mass destruction: siege and starvation. Below the monitor, three guys are playing pool.

All the others, at the tables, are chatting. Laughing and drinking beer.

On the screen these gaunt bodies. Skeletal. Invisible.

I chose Amsterdam because, though it's true it doesn't have a lake, it has all these canals, all these cafés. And maybe one day, I thought—maybe one day I'll find the same radiant light as that time in Piediluco. And partly because I don't know anyone here. And right now, "*I cannot get on with . . . people*"—any question, any topic seems pointless. Utterly pointless. *"He wants me to tell him about the front [but] I realise he does not know that a man cannot talk of such things."* Then again. *All Quiet on the Western Front.*[*]

At Waterstone's, the English bookshop, the only book on Syria is an anthology of articles by Marie Colvin. "You do a great job," my landlord tells me as he explains the keypads for the heating, for the bicycle alarm. "Without people like you, we would have no idea what's happening in the world. You must be proud," he says. "Your work is vital." His wife comes in. "Do you know this girl is from Aleppo?" "Aleppo?" she says. "Are you Iraqi?" "No, no," he says. "Syria. She's in Syria. You wouldn't think so, right? So young . . . She's embedded with the Americans."

The UN announced today that it will no longer count the dead. It says its sources are unreliable, the count is too tricky. And so, instead of putting an end to the war, it's putting an end to the body count. At 130,000. As for the rest, not only won't they have a name, but they won't even be a number.

One hundred thirty thousand deaths, nearly 2.5 million refugees, 7 million people displaced. The UN has asked for 6.5 billion dollars for a humanitarian tragedy which, it warns, is devastating neighboring countries one by one. There is fighting in Lebanon now, and street-by-street hostilities in Tripoli, in the north, which is divided between Sunnis and Alawites like a small-scale Syria. Refugees make up 20 percent of the population in a country that was already collapsing on its own. While in Geneva they're planning a peace conference. With Russia and the United States. With the regime and the official opposition, the European Union, Turkey, and

---

[*] Remarque, op. cit., 165.

Saudi Arabia. With Indonesia, Mexico, Luxembourg, even South Korea.

But without Iran. And without the rebels.

Who are too engaged, at the moment, to go to Geneva.

All the Syrians can do is die or run. And often they die anyway, like the 366, not counting the missing, who drowned on October 3, 2013, off the shore of Lampedusa. The dead were granted honorary Italian citizenship. The living were sent back.

Of the 2.5 million refugees registered at the United Nations, 97 percent were admitted from neighboring countries. Europe, in December 2013, took in fourteen thousand refugees. No, that's not a misprint. It's really fourteen thousand. Eleven thousand of which went to Germany. Britain, the country that most wanted to intervene, that supposedly cared the most about Syria, took in zero refugees.

And now that Assad feels stronger than before—now that he knows that no one will bomb him, that all he has to do is refrain from using gas—it's easy to get a visa to go to Damascus again. And once more we have these articles describing life as usual, restaurants, cafés—articles that assure you that everything is normal under the regime, everything but the economic crisis: "Unemployment is beginning to be felt here too, you know? The other day I was at the gym and someone stole my iPhone."

Six miles from Moadamiya.

The first photos from Moadamiya continue to arrive punctually, every morning at five. And they show skeletons. The one in today's image is chewing cardboard. They've eaten cats, dogs, leaves. Rats. Roots. There's nothing left. Only skeletons, nothing more. "We sit in silence all day," they write to you, "because talking consumes calories."

Moadamiya.

I call a UN official. "But no, look," he tells me, "technically we can't talk about starvation. We detect cases of food insecurity, of course, a widespread uneasiness, but no, the term isn't appropriate. We can't call it starvation."

But we can call you a dickhead.

Moadamiya.

Meanwhile I'm here and this city—this city is so strange. I listen to a debate about the Left and the prospects of the peace movement. The question is why did we mobilize for Bosnia, for Iraq, and not for Syria? Of the three speakers, one begins with Rosa Luxemburg, the other with the contradictions of capitalism. The third wonders whether the rebels lack the functional equivalent of a working class consciousness. And the problem is: if we support the rebels, we support Al Qaeda. Whom, however, we are fighting in Pakistan. The enemy of my friend is my enemy, but what if the friend of my friend is my enemy? Is the friend of my enemy my friend? And what about the cousin of the enemy of the enemy of my friend? And why don't we talk about the factories of Bangladesh anymore? In that box to the left, a euro to send blankets to the refugees, thank you.

Meanwhile.

Meanwhile I read the mail as I listen: Mohammed Noor was kidnapped by Al Qaeda today, and my last fixer was killed by a mortar along with my last interpreter. Whose daughter has meanwhile pronounced her first word: "MIG."

But it's not true that no one is interested in Syria.

They invited me to come on RAI 1 for a reality show starring broke showgirls, singers, and TV personalities living among the refugees.

Meanwhile I wander around Amsterdam, and Amsterdam is beautiful.

Meanwhile I see myself reflected in the windows of the shops, of the cafés with all those people inside.

Life.

I look at my reflection in the water.

Amsterdam.

In the end I left too.

We all left. And yet it's not that the war in Syria became more dangerous. By and large, it wasn't much better a year ago, when Aleppo was one fierce explosion every six seconds, the wounded with no time for a last breath before a mortar pulverized them. Except that we were with the rebels then, and the rebels, no matter how stricken, were fighting for freedom. And we were there to bear witness, to show the world Assad's crimes. Now that Aleppo is starving, however, nothing but hunger and sharia, women covered up Afghan-style and malnourished children, now that a new regime has replaced the old, we've suddenly discovered what war means when you are not embedded. Now we are here to attest, to show the world the rebels' crimes as well, and both the rebels and the regime hunt us as enemies.

This war hasn't become more dangerous, only more real.

And now that for us, too, the war is what it has always been for civilians, a war in which no one is innocent, no one is immune, a war in which no one is welcome—we all got out.

It was February 2012 when I decided that I would write about Syria. When I saw those photographs in *Time*. In the hospitals in Tripoli, in Lebanon, the Homs survivors who had housed, helped, and protected Alessio limped toward him, moved: finally Syria was on the front pages. Now they capture us. Why? What changed since that day in Tripoli?

Don't we have responsibilities here? We're journalists, our role is to ask questions. Why are we in the crosshairs? Maybe because so many were here just for the money, for a single feature, a single photo, an award, a contract, and so for the Syrians we became a trade, a business like any other? Maybe because, when Abdallah, who made the work possible for so many of us, was killed, no one left a flower on his grave, not after he'd defended us and enabled the arrest of two kidnappers? Maybe because all we wrote about was blood, blood, blood, because it was easier, because it was less expensive, giving the world a misleading portrait of Syria, a grainy picture that now generates uncertain and confused policies? Maybe because we flocked to the border by the dozens after the chemical attack, only to disappear, disappointed, when Obama chose not to bomb?

Maybe because, whether we're here or not, it's all the same to the Syrians? Because to them we are merely the reflection and expression of the international community and its cynicism?

Our role is to ask questions. Even of ourselves.

I was reading the usual email a few nights ago, "No thanks, beautiful reportage, but not interested in Aleppo," and I was on Twitter when a plane roared overhead. In a second, everyone followed me—all of them, I'm afraid, waiting for my last tweet from under the rubble. And my reaction, since I was more than a journalist at that moment—I was just like any other person with a plane over her head and death at her door—my only reaction was: go to hell.

And I shut down.

Now here we are with our Hostile Environment Awareness Training (HEAT), borrowed from the military as if we too were in the army. Only—only words are important, aren't they? He who speaks evil, thinks evil. And commits evil.

Syria is not a hostile environment. It's a dangerous and complex environment, and so, of course, training is essential: but it is not hostile. Because we aren't here to oppose an enemy. Everyone thinks it's about money. About money and strength. But there are things that cannot be bought. Like respect. You have to build human relationships, not contractual ones. Because that's the only real safety in situations like this: social protection.

But here we are. Studying the history of the Kalashnikov, not the history of Syria. Learning how to survive in the jungle. "Threats" my manual lists in the first chapter: "1. The locals often do not speak English." The problem, if anything, is that we don't speak Arabic.

Meanwhile I wander around Amsterdam and can only say of my last two years: a failure. Two years, and readers barely remember where Damascus is. Barely remember who Assad is. Because it was a war for freelance journalists—and now they're all in Cairo, and from Cairo they will then all go to Kiev. All covering the countries that cost less, and increasingly, countries that you can enter without a visa, since to obtain a visa you often have to indicate the publication for which you write, and no one will now commission a piece from you. If you get killed, no one wants to be responsible. And so no one writes about the Central African Republic. About South Sudan. Bahrain. Chechnya. And how can you build relationships, step by step, how can you win trust, respect, in Syria, when even the best newspapers now have only one correspondent each for the entire Middle East? Buy a paper, even one of the best publications, and it reads like a low-cost daily; and it's not just the war reporting. Because no piece requires as much resourcefulness as an investigative report—let's report what's possible, not what's important. Let's write only about the front, only about those who are fighting. Any revolution, thus, becomes a war. Their freedom depended on us too.

The news is homogenized by descriptive articles that don't cite police records, how many died and where, or what caused the deaths. What's more important when you're writing about a sniper? How many victims he struck, or that car parked in front of the door as if he's at the office? What explains a war more? What the hell are we, stenographers or journalists? Does Syria really only speak of Sunnis and Shiites, the rebels and the regime? Does it really have nothing else to say to us? We aren't notaries.

That rubble, is it really just about Aleppo?

And while it was all so difficult, the regime, the rebels, the Islamists, the publishers, and the editors—not only weren't we journalists able to work together—but we all thwarted one another. I thought I had seen it all after a colleague sent me into the snipers just so she could finish first in the cavalcade. But the evening before I entered Aleppo, this last time, a reporter from the U.S. called half of Antakya to have the Free Army stop me—because he'd been there for ten days and couldn't get in, and how would it make him look now, a man who has won dozens of awards, to be beaten by a girl? In the end you go to Syria and the danger is not just Al Qaeda, not just missiles, not just bullets: the danger is other journalists.

And maybe worst of all, my mother was sick these past two years. One of those illnesses where you wander from doctor to doctor, from treatment to treatment, and no one knows what it is. And in the evening, when I was on the phone with her, when I didn't need to explain how I felt being in Syria— in two years no one ever asked me how my mother was.

Or how I was.

Lorenzo Milani wrote: "My neighbor is not Africa, not the proletariat, but those around me."* And if you're not able to ask the person living beside you how she is, how on earth would you ever be able to write about Syria?

All I can say about my last two years: a failure.

Yesterday Molhem Barakat was killed. Reuters had bought him a Canon, but not a helmet. Not a bulletproof vest. He was seventeen years old. And so he died, a child photographer, while we were looking for a child soldier. Sent to the front for ten dollars a photo.

That rubble, is it really just Aleppo?

Every time. "There's nothing to write about." Yet each time, you come back, and you find you've crossed another red line: from gunfire to aircraft, from planes to missiles, from typhus to leishmaniasis, from leishmaniasis to polio, even now as I'm writing. I'm writing about Moadamiya and already there's a hunger crisis in Ghouta as well. I reread what I have written and already there is a hunger crisis in Yarmouk too. And then from hunger we have already moved on to an even more economical weapon, more capable of mass destruction, and even swifter: explosive barrels. Barrels. Filled with nails and dynamite. An average of thirty barrels a day. A thousand deaths a day. As many as a chemical attack, every day. Then again, now that people no longer die from gas but from everything else in Syria, nobody cares.

Nobody. Except you keep getting these messages: "They're

---

* Lorenzo Milani Comparetti, known simply as don Milani, was a Roman Catholic priest, best known as an educator of poor children and an advocate of conscientious objection. The phrase quoted is from his collection of letters entitled *Lettere al mio prossimo* (Letters to My Neighbor).

killing us all!" Hour after hour, minute after minute, "Where are you? Where are you?"

I don't know. I don't know where we are, I don't know. My most read piece, in these two years, was my piece on freelance reporters: the only piece that doesn't talk about Syria. And every comment, every criticism ducks responsibility—I called that UN official first, I needed some data, and he said: "But it was the American, right?" Because I had tweeted that thing about "starvation." An inappropriate term. "It was the American, wasn't it?" he said. "That guy is just an asshole." And each time you're tempted to yell: "I was talking about *you*! I was referring to you! You are the asshole! I was talking about you!" Every time. They all think you're not talking about them. But no. I was talking about you. You in particular.

About us in particular.

And yet . . . *when I speak,*
my words remain in the air
like corks on water.*

Kevin Carter was my age. Thirty-three years old. He took this photo in Sudan, a child on the ground with a vulture behind him. During the famine. He took the photo and went away, because they had told him not to touch the children, not to touch anyone, that he might catch something. So he took the photo and left. No one heard anything more about that child.

They tried to trace him, but no one could.

Kevin Carter won the Pulitzer with that photo.

---

* Federico García Lorca, "Afternoon. November 1919," *Book of Poems (Selection)/Libro de poemas (Selección): A Dual-Language Book*, trans. and ed. Stanley Appelbaum (Mineola, NY: Dover Publications, 2004), 71.

Three months later he committed suicide.

I think of him, in the evening.

While Amsterdam is so beautiful. So offensive, while Aleppo is dying.

While I write my book. I think I understand him.

While I gaze at the houses. At the night, the lights. I stare at the lights in other people's homes. And all those lives, so normal, so appealing, those lives that will never be mine.

While they tell you: "You've been translated into nine languages. Now a book. Two extraordinary years," they say. And you ask them: "Who is Assad? And the rebels? Who are they? What do they want?" And nobody knows anything. "Do you know she's come from Aleppo?" "Aleppo? But wasn't Gaddafi killed? I thought the war was over." "No, no, that one is in Libya. She's in Syria. She's with the Taliban."

Two years and no one knows anything.

I don't even know what's happening on the other side of Aleppo.

And, meanwhile, the Syrians I have written about in this book are all dead.

In Aleppo they're fighting again. Because while the rebels clean out the shops, empty the houses, the factories, while they resell the copper from electric cables, while they resell even the metal water piping, and while the Islamists focus on the caliphate, Assad is back on the offensive. His men have finally broken through the resistance in the southeast, at al-Safirah. It was the base of Liwa al-Tawhid, the chief brigade in Aleppo. And from al-Safirah, in a few hours, the battle has flared again. Colonel al-Okaidi, commander of the Free Army, has resigned. For once, al-Okaidi admitted, it wasn't a matter of a lack of weapons and ammunition: Liwa al-Tawhid was engaged north of Aleppo, not against Assad's troops, he decried, but against other rebels.

On the other hand. At Wadi Deif, in Idlib province, Jamal Maarouf's men have continued fighting for months, each time stopping a moment before the regime's troops surrender, in order to go on receiving funds from their Gulf backers.

While explosive barrels rain down. A thousand deaths a day and there is no shelter. Everyone tries to flee, but the rebels are fighting with Islamists at the border over control of the supply routes and arms smuggling, so the border is closed.

"Where are you? They're killing us all! They're killing us all! Where are you?"

We've all left, one by one. Gone.

And me too.

I'm here now, trying to write, to report, but I'm jumpy, I get up every five minutes, I read, make a call, distract myself, looking for an excuse to pause, to defer, to run from the page time after time, because once you've written you can no longer forget, once you've seen you cannot unsee. These two months here have been harder than my two years in Syria, and I definitely feel out of place, now that I no longer have anywhere to return to, now that even Ramallah is not my home, now that exile is permanent and now that I really am Palestinian, they were right, and I really am Jewish. There is no return, and so I pedal, I pedal swiftly around this city, the music of Radiohead or U2 in my headphones, in search of a light that I can't find now that I've lost everything, and so I pedal, I pedal swiftly, only this, head down to dodge the snipers as Aleppo lies in wait behind every noise, every shadow, every flash an explosion, every clack of a woman's heels the sharp report of a sniper, and it's no use, it sounds like an incoming plane—it will always be an incoming plane—but it's only a gate sliding shut, now that everything is reduced to rubble, and I pedal, pedal, pedal swiftly, no longer knowing where to go, with nothing to go back to anymore, and I try to keep going, but every corner, around every corner of the entire city, there's another city behind the city, an echo in every voice, while to my right, suddenly, the World Press Photo center runs by me and I think about April, I think about the day of the awards ceremony, how everyone was looking at those photos, Gaza, Syria, Afghanistan, all the wars, all the dead, and they were all there discussing contrast, color, framing, the latest Nikon, among the dead, and how, from the stage, all Alessio said was: "I am ashamed."

Now that life is more frightening than Syria.

"**S**till going on about that story? They're where they were a year ago!" Lorenzo told me predictably from Kiev. "Let them tell their own story! It's their war—what the hell do you want with Syria?"

I'm back at the border. Since my last time here, no one has been able to get into Aleppo anymore. More exactly: no one has come back. In three years, sixty-two journalists have been killed. I'm here waiting for a Saudi commander to give the green light. The problem is to avoid a regime checkpoint controlled by Iranians, but everything has been arranged now. The fixer is a Tunisian, and I'll even have Internet. At the base of a group of Afghans. The interpreter came from Amsterdam, like me.

There's no one left in Syria. Not even Syrians.

Because for three months now, explosive barrels have been raining down. All day, all night: tons and tons of nails and dynamite. They have the power of aviation, but the frequency of artillery—and the Syrians gave in. Terrified, they poured into Turkey by the thousands. We have no idea how many dead there are, but the latest estimates say 150,000, plus 250,000 so-called secondary deaths, that is, those who technically did not die as a direct result of the war, but because cancer, even now—even in Damascus, where journalists friendly to the regime, the only ones who can get a visa, assure us that everything is normal, that life goes on as usual in Syria, maybe just in the morning, to shower, you know? the water is a little cold—even in Damascus, cancer today is treated with herbs and teas.

To those who for months have had nothing but leaves and roots for supper, the only meat that of stray cats, to those who, depleted, chew cardboard so as not to black out, even the flu is lethal.

Negotiations in Geneva, meanwhile, have failed. So to speak. More precisely, they were discontinued. Because they couldn't even reach agreement on the reasons for the failure. At a certain point the delegates simply left and never came back.

Nevertheless, faced with photos of skeletons under siege, the NGOs and UN agencies have finally mobilized. They're still at the border, still here where they can only assist refugees: only those who manage to flee Syria on their own. A truly noteworthy undertaking, since refugees now number two and a half million. And represent only one-third of the more than nine million Syrians who no longer have a home—though at least now they're struggling as hard as they can to go back. Assad, however, doesn't respond: he's busy with the elections, the vote is in June. He re-nominated himself for president. While the rebels decided to regroup. Too many brigades, they said, too much anarchy: everyone here does as he pleases. So they appointed a new commander. But when asked at his first interview if the rebels would finally stop kidnapping everyone now, he said: "Can I call you back in five minutes?" He wasn't aware that he was head of the Free Army.

He said he had to check a minute. To hear it on the news.

The explosive barrels are so deadly that I thought Aleppo would fall. But it's been this way for months. The rebels seemingly about to win, advancing and advancing. Then, abruptly, the weapons stop coming. And the regime goes on the offensive at that point, seemingly about to win, advancing and advancing. Then suddenly new weapons reach the rebels.

At the beginning some analysts, especially in the U.S., advised: "Let them butcher each other." Hezbollah, Iran. Al Qaeda. Let them kill each other. Let them use their weapons against themselves, instead of against Israel. Against us.

Did we really just watch? Not intervene?

Is this really not our war?

Meanwhile, even now, all I get are these messages. Every day. Where are you?

They're killing us all! Day after day, hour after hour—Where are you?

Three years later, however, it's not true that things are still the same here. Now they no longer tell me: "There's nothing to write about." Now they say: "But you've finished the book, why the hell do you still care about Syria?"

— Antakya, March 30, 2014

Since the fighting started in August 2012, since the rebels of the Free Army began their offensive, only one thing hasn't changed here. The only anti-aircraft protection is bad weather.

The only refuge is luck.

Over these months I've written about a city reduced to rubble. About bursts of mortars, streets peppered with snipers, missiles and bomb blasts, I described a city disfigured by typhus, by leishmaniasis, by starvation, I wrote of children who look like they're in Ethiopia or Somalia, the skin on their bones like wax, their supper grass and rainwater. I wrote about rivers spewing corpses, clouds of insects on the remains of an intestine, a liver, a lung; about grenades, rockets, fighter planes, beheaded activists, executed fifteen-year-olds. In hospitals being bombed, I saw kitchen knives used as scalpels, a nurse's touch the only anesthetic; I saw mutilated bodies, heads, hands, fingers, skull fragments lying on chairs.

150,000 confirmed dead, 220,000 estimated. I wrote about horror, over these months, about dismay, brutality, savagery. Pain. I used every possible word.

Exhausted every adjective.

Sorry. I still didn't know what war was.

Assad's counter-offensive began in December 2013. You enter the city through ten miles of front line now, starting from the industrial zone of Sheikh Najjar, once so tightly controlled by the rebels that it housed the headquarters of the Revolutionary Council, Aleppo's provisional government which optimistically planned to restore pipes, reopen schools, even replant trees. Instead you now race full speed through mortars, RPGs, Kalashnikovs, a plane buzzing overhead, to get to shelter as fast as possible in the residential neighborhoods. That is, under explosive barrels. Barrels. Barrels filled with gasoline and dynamite, hurled down from choppers two, three, four at a time. They rain down by the dozens, every day, every night, every hour, everywhere, literally everywhere, an average of fifty per day. And no distinction is made between civilians and combatants. The only difference is that the front is bombed with planes, which are more precise. As usual, rebels and loyalists are so close that they shout insults as they shoot at one another; the barrels would hit the loyalists as well. But that's the only difference. Because other than that, there is only one criterion for distinguishing and selecting targets in Aleppo: clockwise or counterclockwise.

We continue to call it that. Aleppo. But by now it's Dresden.

Miles and miles—Aleppo no longer exists. Each day more and more rubble.

Yet it's not as deserted as it seems. As they say. Because becoming a refugee, as my interpreter remarks, "is a luxury that not everyone can afford." Not everyone has $150 to pay for a car to get to Turkey, plus $100 a head, for a wife and three kids, to bribe a police officer and cross the border illegally. Only a few still have a passport. And in any case there are now seven hundred thousand refugees in Turkey: the UN camps are a shambles. Aleppo seems deserted, but hundreds of people, thousands, shattered, are still here.

Eighty thousand, according to estimates. Chewing cardboard to ease their hunger, looking consumed, haggard, standing by the roadside in tatters, gazing up at the sky— because at one time a plane would come and bomb two, three times a week, it would bomb and disappear, but now a chopper hovers overhead and bombs without warning, two, three times an hour. All of a sudden you die. That's all you can do in Aleppo. Nothing else. You wait and you die, in this hornet's nest, this nest of rumbling booms, that's all, just the roaring that grows louder at times, only this scream, suddenly, *tayara! tayara!*, a plane!, and everyone ducks under a chair, behind a cabinet, a vase, a bucket, anything—because Aleppo looks deserted, and instead they materialize from the rubble before you by the hundreds, by the thousands, terrified. They live like this, in the midst of bodies that were never recovered. Thinking that maybe a house that's already been hit is less likely to be hit again. Scattered amid the stones, amid the concrete slabs: clothes, books, a clock, a shoe with a child's foot still inside. "To you we're nothing but a number," a young man in Sayf al-Dawla protests as he insists on dictating to me the list of victims from the last bombing. Name by name. But as of January, the UN stopped recording the death toll: too difficult to update, the sources, he explained, are unreliable— and so, instead of stopping the war, they've stopped tracking the death toll. The young man protests, he insists on telling me their story, one by one. He doesn't know that to us the dead in Syria are no longer even a number.

But talking, asking questions in Aleppo is difficult. And not just because journalists are still being targeted by Al Qaeda, still forced to go around undercover, as invisible as possible—at the moment, more than twenty of us are missing without a trace. Talking is difficult because the Syrians try to answer you, men, women, young and old, anyone: they start to speak, say a few words, but then they collapse on your shoulder in despair—and weep. They weep, and it's they who ask the question—why? Why? they ask you, and they can't say anything more, despairing. They hug you and weep.

They weep until the next explosion. Until a Dushka coughs out four, five rounds: not to defend you, not to bring it down, just to warn you that in a few seconds a chopper will arrive, a few seconds and maybe you'll die, and once again now you too hear the roar, louder and louder, closer, in those infinite few seconds, and they're all screaming again, running again—and again, viciously, the explosion. You hold your breath. Al-Ansari, 4:40 p.m. The first to emerge is the shadow of a woman. Penetrating the fog of dust and cordite, she staggers toward you. Then a man, another figure, yet another, someone falls unconscious, these limp, incomprehensible bodies in people's arms, these torn bodies, bleeding, dripping on the ground. The child you came across a short time before is now lying there, ashen, still clutching his teddy bear.

A rug, a fan, a torso scattered about. A tricycle.

And for days, at dawn, in silhouette, you see women bent over this shoreline of human remains, as if searching for seashells. Between their fingers a scrap of cloth, a remnant of a child.

You die in Aleppo. That's it. You wait and you die.

They're on their own, the Syrians, completely alone, on this side of the red line—here where you don't die from gas, but from everything else. And so nobody cares. Those displaced amount to 9 million, almost half the population. And 3.5 million are in areas that the UN defines as "dangerous to reach."

The imams, in November, authorized the cooking of stray cats.

Despite the fact that Security Council Resolution 2139, adopted on February 22, 2014, demands that delivery of humanitarian aid not be obstructed, for now the UN—which by statute operates through the only recognized government, namely the Assad government—chooses not to enforce it. And to conform. Assad prohibits aid convoys from entering via the Turkish border, which is controlled by the rebels, forcing them to enter much further south, with time, costs, and risks up to ten times greater, Human Rights Watch accuses. Worst of all, with so many restrictions on movement that nearly all of the aid, 90 percent, ends up in areas under the regime's control. The regime claims that it is to ensure the safety of the humanitarian workers, but the story told by the Red Cross, whose files are complete with names and photos, is somewhat different. The regime has arrested and tortured many of those who tried to reach areas under rebel control.

Those who did manage to reach them, however, were seized by Al Qaeda.

In theory, some convoys are said to have entered in recent days, but no one in Aleppo seems to have received anything. Rice, sugar. You never come across anything here that has a foreign logo. A bottle of milk. Anything. The only thing you can be sure of is that when you're embedded with the rebels— no matter which of the more than a thousand groups they are now split into—food is never lacking. In fact, the Islamists, and in particular the young men from the European suburbs who land here with beard and iPad, acclaim Syria on Facebook as "a five-star jihad," promising potential recruits that they won't find a new Mali, nothing but hunger and sand.

The only other certainty here is the fact that the sole area in Aleppo that has never been bombed is Al Qaeda's headquarters. And it's the same elsewhere in Syria. Because of the compound's isolated location, it is strictly speaking the only lawful military target—the only one that could be hit without collateral damage disproportionate to the military advantage gained. Yet it's still there.

And it's the same in other parts of Syria.

Except for Al Qaeda, everything is under attack. "By now it's no longer a question of humanitarian aid," says Moayed Zarnaji, a Red Cross volunteer. "A kilo of rice won't make any difference. You'll die anyway." Often, you'll die anyway even if you survive the bombing: no one will come to pull you out of the rubble. They have a Civil Defense unit now, guys with flashlights, gloves, plastic helmets, a tractor, sort of like a fire department.

There are about thirty of them, but the number varies from day to day, from hour to hour. Because the corpses, in Aleppo, are always in pairs: the second one being the person who instinctively runs to help and is hit by the second barrel. And even if they pull you out of the rubble, no one here has anything to treat you with anymore. Only two hospitals are left. Actually, only one: the other was hit as I was writing. "Even if they treat you, you go back under the helicopters," a little girl tells me. Her left arm is all splinters and scars. Before she can show me her right arm, a mortar explodes, down the street, and she runs away.

Because you wait and you die in Aleppo. That's all.

And nothing is more atrocious than the first bombing.
When someone, under there, is still alive, and you hear the
voices, the screams, amid the dust, while you still can't dis-
tinguish anything, *saa'idni! saaa'idni!*, they implore you, help
me!, help me! Like this woman, now. We are in Soukkari,
hearing the shrieks of her two grandchildren, seventeen and
eighteen years old, relatives restraining her as she struggles
to break free, and falls, gets up, screams, *saa'idni! saaa'idni!*, and
it's the cruelest moment, brothers, fathers, friends, everyone
restraining them as they struggle to break free, desperate,
clawing at the rubble, like that, with their bare hands, and
right away, another chopper promptly arrives, hovers sadis-
tically as everyone runs, yet again, and now, no one knows
where to run anymore, everyone struggling, falling, scram-
bling back up, amid the screams, the clatter of the blades, the
dust, the blood—the explosion.

Because you die, in Aleppo. That's all.

The city is divided in two: half under rebel control, half
under the control of the regime. And in the eastern sector, the
rebel half, a new regime, that of Al Qaeda, replaced the old
one in September. But today it no longer even makes sense
to talk about a regime here; it's the rebels or Assad. Because
Aleppo is, simply, a no-man's-land. Prey to criminal gangs.
Checkpoints have essentially disappeared: the rebels are all
at the front, embroiled in fighting. After spending more time
looting and extorting than governing the city, and above all,
after having destroyed each other in internal clashes, thereby
paving the way for Assad's counter-offensive, they are now
engaged in cutting off supply routes with Damascus, as well
as carrying out a diversionary operation in the southwest, in

the province of Latakia. Our analysts follow military developments step by step, map in hand: who's advancing, who's falling back, hour after hour. But no matter who advances, no matter who falls back, in reality no one is governing anything here—it's life in the wild. No one controls anyone anymore.

There's nothing left to capture but rubble.

The only visible sign of authority is at the entrance to Karaj al-Hajez, more commonly known as "the Death Crossing" because it is the crossing point between the two halves of Aleppo and is under constant fire from Assad's snipers. For those who live in the eastern half, it's essential, since for many, a great many, the only source of income is their state employee wages, which must be earned in the western side. That or selling fruit, vegetables, meat, because prices are higher in the west and you can sell a pound there to buy two here. But most importantly, in the west you are not under bombardment. And you have humanitarian aid. Those who have been displaced are all over there. And so the only visible sign of authority is here, at the Karaj al-Hajez crossing. Earlier the Islamists of Al Qaeda had banned the transport of food. Now they've built a wall.

Syrians no longer argue over politics. The war, now fought mainly by foreigners—jihadists on the one hand, Hezbollah, Iranians, and assorted mercenaries on the other—no longer seems to interest them. They no longer talk about "liberated areas." Now it's simply East Aleppo and West Aleppo.

"The Free Army advances and advances, it seems to be about to win—then, all of a sudden, no more weapons arrive. And the regime goes on the counter-offensive. The regime advances, advances, seems about to win—and suddenly the Free Army gets new weapons. And it's been that way for months," Alaa Alloush recaps the situation. He's one of the last activists still here. Still alive. "You're all there debating the advisability of outside intervention. But outside intervention here is already underway. What we need instead is an internal intervention, so that Syria may be returned to us Syrians."

Because the only priority here is survival. Helicopters, airplanes, airplanes, helicopters: there's no respite. And in the evening all you can do is huddle in a corner, terrified. On local television, *Aleppo Today*, the list of dead streams by constantly, like final credits, at the bottom of the screen, while outside the window, in the dark, every ten, twenty, thirty minutes, the specter of Aleppo reappears in the flash of an explosion. I keep looking nervously at my watch. Waiting for dawn. But I'm the only one: it's a habit from another life. Because the only difference between night and day here is that at night you can't even run away. At night the war in Aleppo becomes slaughter. You don't fight: you die and that's it. Randomly.

Because they bomb here, they bomb and bomb and bomb. That's all.

AUTHOR'S NOTE AND
ACKNOWLEDGMENTS

I have changed the names and identifying characteristics of certain individuals who are described here in terms that are less than flattering, that is, those who might in the coming months be tempted to pursue me throughout the entire Middle East with a pitchfork. Repetitions are not typographical errors but the most explicit way I had to express the senselessness of this war—months and months of it—when the only thing on the ground that changed were the names; only the number of dead advanced.

The story of Qannaas, on pages 25–29, is an adaptation of a piece by Rania Abouzeid, an Australian of Lebanese origin who has written about Syria better than anyone else, in my opinion. I think that one of the major mistakes we journalists make in Syria is an utter failure to collaborate. For me, journalism is not an individual endeavor but a collective undertaking, to which everyone contributes a fragment of understanding. Which is why I wanted to include a piece by Rania Abouzeid in my book. For one thing, because her crosshairs focused on targets that are so worthy of note. And because this is how I wish journalism could be: less narcissistic, less egocentric. Less focused on awards and more focused on readers. On what best enables readers to understand. And so my thanks to Rania Abouzeid.

My thanks as well to Roberto Saviano for his reference to Philip Roth and Primo Levi, on page 35.

Thanks to Christian Raimo, who first saw a book in my notes. And thank you to Stefano Citati, who first saw a journalist in me, and to Yuri Kozyrev, who with a look, in Amsterdam, taught me what it means to be one.

My thanks to the Israelis and Palestinians. Always.

And my gratitude to Claudio Romenzi, for pulling me to the ground one morning in September.

ABOUT THE AUTHOR

FRANCESCA BORRI was born in Italy in 1980. She holds a
bachelor's degree in philosophy of law, and master's degrees in
international relations and human rights. After working for a
nongovernmental organization in the Balkans, she transferred
to the Middle East where she was a human rights officer. She
turned to journalism in February 2012 to cover the war in Syria.
She is the author of two earlier books, one on Kosovo that was
published in 2008, the other on Israel and Palestine, published
in 2010. *Syrian Dust* is her first book to be translated into English.

ABOUT THE TRANSLATOR

ANNE MILANO APPEL, PHD, was awarded the Italian Prose in Translation Award (2015), the John Florio Prize for Italian Translation (2013), and the Northern California Book Awards for Translation–Fiction (2014, 2013). She has translated works by Claudio Magris, Paolo Giordano, and Giovanni Arpino, among others. Forthcoming titles include works by Roberto Saviano and Giuseppe Catozzella.

ABOUT SEVEN STORIES PRESS

SEVEN STORIES PRESS is an independent book publisher based in New York City. We publish works of the imagination by such writers as Nelson Algren, Russell Banks, Octavia E. Butler, Ani DiFranco, Assia Djebar, Ariel Dorfman, Coco Fusco, Barry Gifford, Martha Long, Luis Negrón, Hwang Sok-yong, Lee Stringer, and Kurt Vonnegut, to name a few, together with political titles by voices of conscience, including Subhankar Banerjee, the Boston Women's Health Collective, Noam Chomsky, Angela Y. Davis, Human Rights Watch, Derrick Jensen, Ralph Nader, Loretta Napoleoni, Gary Null, Greg Palast, Project Censored, Barbara Seaman, Alice Walker, Gary Webb, and Howard Zinn, among many others. Seven Stories Press believes publishers have a special responsibility to defend free speech and human rights, and to celebrate the gifts of the human imagination, wherever we can. In 2012 we launched Triangle Square books for young readers with strong social justice and narrative components, telling personal stories of courage and commitment. For additional information, visit www.sevenstories.com.